Crochet
ANIMAL
SLIPPERS

IRA ROTT

DAVID & CHARLES

www.davidandcharles.com

Contents

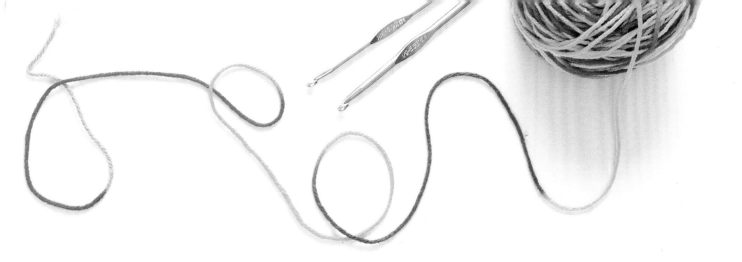

Welcome

Ever since I was a little girl, my mom and grandma have often spoiled me with their handmade slippers and socks. Sometimes it feels that time goes by very quickly, but those precious memories and handmade with love creations never fade away from my heart. So I was inspired to design a book of crochet patterns for making adorable cozy slippers that bring smiles, joy and happiness.

This book includes more than 20 fun animal designs from around the globe: Safari animals, marsupials and mammals, giant pandas from the bamboo forests, woodland creatures, prehistoric dinosaurs and reptiles, barn animals and our best pets – cats and dogs.

You can create several different looks from each animal design by using different types of slippers – Shoes, Boots or Slides. In addition, you can use my bonus pattern for basic toe-up slippers to finish beginner level animals. Let your creativity shine by mixing and matching patterns and make over 60 pairs of adorable animal slippers from just one book!

All patterns come in a variety of sizes, ranging from Small Kids (aged 4+) to Large Adults. I hope you will enjoy making them for your little ones, friends, family and of course, for yourself.

Whether you're new to crochet or have many years of experience, you can find projects that will suit your skills. Don't worry about stepping out of your comfort zone to try something new. Crochet is a fun and easy art so just be yourself and happy crafting!

Ira Rott

Happy Crafting!

How to Use This Book

SKILL LEVELS

Each pattern in this book has been assigned a level of difficulty based on the crochet stitches and techniques used for creating these designs – Beginner (1), Easy (2) and Moderate (3). Pick a pattern that suits your skill level, and then move up to the next level as you get comfortable with your projects.

● ○ ○ ○

BEGINNER – The best choice for novice crocheters. These patterns include basic crochet stitches and techniques with minimal shaping, simple repeats and easy assembly.

● ● ○ ○

EASY – These patterns have basic stitches and easy assembly, as well as some unique, yet easy to learn stitches: front/back post double crochet (fpdc/bpdc), reverse single crochet (rsc) and picot. Simple repeats may include instructions for multiple sizes written using parentheses.

● ● ● ○

MODERATE – In these patterns you will find a few challenging stitches and techniques such as loop stitch (lp), popcorn stitch (PC) and working short rows. Some parts of assembly might also be more challenging.

SIZES

We included six sizes in this book, ranging from Small Kids (aged 4+) to Large Adults. The sizes are determined by the length and width of the foot (*see Size Chart*).

Instructions for different sizes are written using parentheses – S (M, L). The number before parentheses is given for the smallest size and the numbers in parentheses are for the larger sizes. Example: Ch 8 (10, 12) means – work ch 8 for small size (S), ch 10 for medium size (M) or ch 12 for large size (L). If only one number is given, it applies to all sizes.

GAUGE

The gauge is the numbers of stitches and rounds per 4 x 4in (10 x 10cm) square, which determines the size of your finished slippers. As crochet gauge varies from person to person, it's important to test and achieve the gauge of the pattern for accurate sizing. If you crochet too tightly, your slippers will turn out smaller, or if you crochet too loosely, your slippers will be bigger.

To test your gauge, make a cylinder-shaped swatch by working in the round and count how many stitches and rounds there are per 4in (10cm). You can use a larger or smaller size hook to adjust the gauge if necessary. If you have difficulty getting the right width and height at the same time, the width is your priority.

READING PATTERNS

Crochet patterns in this book are written using American (US) terminology. If you are accustomed to British terminology, you can convert the terms using our conversion chart (*see Useful Information: Terminology*).

- "Work in rows" means – Crochet a row of stitches as indicated in the pattern, then turn your work to begin the next row. The patterns might specify which rows are on right side (RS) and wrong side (WS) when this extra information is helpful or important.
- "Work in the round" means – Begin with a magic ring/foundation ring or work along both sides of the foundation chain. Work with right side (RS) facing you, joining each round with a slip stitch in top of beginning stitch (*see Useful Information: Crochet Techniques*).
- "Work in spiral rounds" means – Begin with a magic ring/foundation ring or work across both sides of the foundation chain (*see Useful Information: Crochet Techniques*). With right side (RS) facing, work the beginning stitch of each round into the first stitch of the previous round without joining. This creates a continuous spiral appearance of the rounds.
- The total stitch count is indicated after the equal sign (=) at the end of each row/round. The beginning chain(s) might be counted as stitch(es) or not, as marked at the beginning of the rows/rounds. Some instructions apply to multiple rows/rounds. Example: Ch 1 (does not count as a st now and throughout).

READING CHARTS

A crochet chart is an illustration created using special symbols to represent stitches and to help you with visualizing patterns. The beginning of the work in charts is marked with a small black arrow. Different colors indicate each row/round along with the row/round number. To understand a chart, refer to the symbol key (*see Useful Information: Abbreviations*). The use of charts is optional. You can choose to follow a chart or a written pattern, or even use both. The charts shown in this book are for right-handed crochet and show your work on the right side (RS). Some charts may begin or end on the wrong side (WS).

Tools and Materials

CROCHET HOOKS

Metric	US Letter	US Number	Canada/UK
3.5mm	E	4	9
3.75mm	F	5	9/8
4.25mm	G	6	8
5mm	H	8	6
5.5mm	I	9	5

NOTE:
If 4.25mm is not available, use 4.5mm (US 7/ Canada and UK 7)

YARN

To make any of these designs, use a single strand of medium weight yarn (weight 4). You can also combine two strands of Super Fine sock yarn (weight 1), just be sure to test the gauge for accuracy. Yarn weight is the thickness of the yarn, which may vary from country to country. Use the following conversion chart to find the correct yarn for your region.

US	UK	Australia	Meters per 100g	Other Terms
Super Fine (1)	4 ply	4 ply	300-400	Fingering/Sock
Medium (4)	Aran	10 ply	150-200	Worsted

The patterns in this book are designed and tested using Bernat Super Value – 100% premium acrylic yarn. We have also tested them using alternative yarns with different fiber contents. Here are some tips for choosing a perfect yarn type for your projects.

- **Acrylic** – 100% premium acrylic yarn is a great choice for all types of slippers. It's durable and easy to care for with a wool-like, even springy texture. This yarn is also the easiest to work with.
- **Wool** – 100% wool or a blend of wool and nylon is perfect for making stretchy Shoes and Boots. This natural yarn is warm, breathable, and holds its shape. For Slides, however, wool is best avoided as it would make them feel small and tricky to slip on.
- **Cotton** – 100% cotton yarn is ideal for Slides. It is very durable, easy to care for and has excellent breathability. However, cotton will stretch out without bouncing back so, while it's good to add a slightly oversized feel to your Slides, it is not suitable for Shoes and Boots as they need to fit more snugly.

ADDITIONAL MATERIALS

- Stitch markers – for marking stitches and indicating the beginning of the rows/rounds
- Tapestry needle – for sewing and weaving in ends
- Sewing needle and thread – for sewing buttons
- Polyester stuffing – used for some designs
- Shelf liner with grip – for making non-slip soles
- Buttons – for eyes: 10mm, 15mm, 20mm
- Craft felt – for highlighting eyes in some designs
- Fabric glue – used for some designs
- Straight pins – for pinning pieces
- Sharp scissors – for cutting yarn and finishing

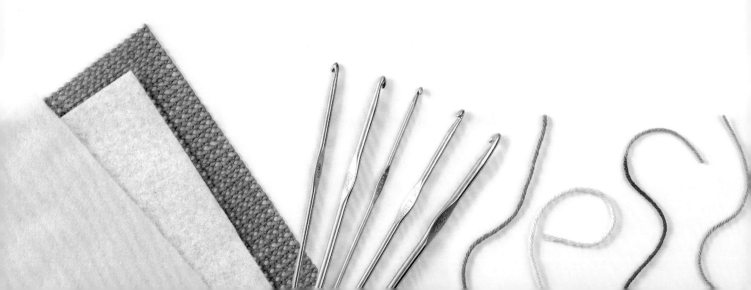

Size Chart

Determine your size based on the length and width of your foot. If the foot is wider than indicated, you can use a larger size hook for the upper of your slippers.

Sizes			Foot Length	Foot Width
KIDS		Small (S)	6¼ - 7in (16 - 18cm)	Up to 3½in (9cm)
		Medium (M)	7 - 7¾in (18 - 19.5cm)	
		Large (L)	7¾ - 8½in (19.5 - 21.5cm)	
ADULTS		Small (S)	8 - 9in (20 - 23cm)	Up to 4in (10cm)
		Medium (M)	9 - 10in (23 - 25.5cm)	
		Large (L)	10 - 11in (25.5 - 28cm)	

HOW TO MEASURE FEET

- Measure while standing on the floor barefoot, or wearing a thin sock. Use a metric or imperial measuring tape/ruler.
- **Foot Length:** Measure from the center of the heel to the end of the longest toe.
- **Foot Width**: Measure across the ball of the foot between the widest points.

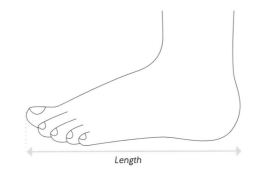

Length

Width

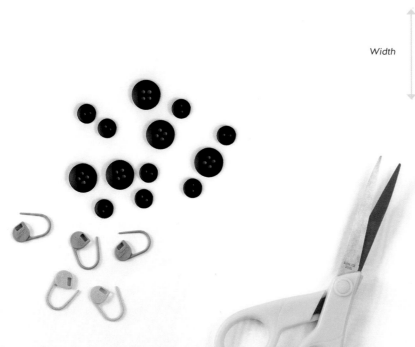

Making Slippers

Shoes - Boots - Slides

Begin your fun adventure of making animal inspired slippers by choosing a base you like.
You can create up to 3 different looks for each animal design, using different types of slippers
(Shoes, Boots, or Slides). If you are a beginner, it might be easier to start with my bonus pattern
for making basic toe-up slippers (*see Additional Ideas*).

SHOES

Shoes are slippers with covered heels

Shoes have negative ease, which means they stretch to fit snugly around
your feet. When choosing materials for this style, consider using a
bouncy yarn with a wool-like texture. The best choice would be a good
quality acrylic yarn or a strong and durable wool yarn. Avoid using
cotton yarns as your Shoes will stretch out instead of fitting snugly (*see
Tools and Materials: Yarn*).

BOOTS

Boots are slippers with ankle cuffs

Boots are made in the same manner as Shoes, but with additional
elements – Ankle Cuffs. Just like Shoes, they are meant to fit snugly and
therefore, the recommended materials are the same as for Shoes.

SLIDES

Slides are backless slippers

For extra comfort and ease of wearing, Slides have a rather loose and
roomy fit compared to Shoes and Boots. Positive ease in this type of
slipper is achieved by using larger size hooks for the soles and upper of
Slides. For the best result, use a good quality acrylic yarn or cotton yarn
(*see Tools and Materials: Yarn*).

Overview

When making slippers, follow the steps in the described order: (1) Gussets, (2) Double-Soles, (3) Upper of Shoes, Boots or Slides.

The gussets and soles are the same for all types of slippers, but the upper is different.

Instructions for different sizes are written using parentheses, where the first number is for the smallest size and the numbers in parentheses are for the following sizes. If only one number is given, it applies to all sizes.

HOOKS

You will be using different hooks for different parts of slippers as indicated in each step.

Type	Hooks		
	Gusset	**Soles**	**Upper of Slippers**
Shoes	4.25mm (G)	5mm (H)	4.25mm (G)
Boots	4.25mm (G)	5mm (H)	4.25mm (G)
Slides	4.25mm (G)	5.5mm (I)	5mm (H)

Stitch Summary:

Ch, sl st, sc, sc2tog or invisible decrease, hdc, dc, bpdc, fpdc, join

Skills:

Working in rows and in the round, raw edge finishing, working across the opposite side of the foundation chain, multiple sizes instructions, working short rows (for Slides only), sewing

Left-Handed Crochet:

See Useful Information: Left-Handed Crochet

GAUGE

Test your gauge by making a cylinder-shaped swatch as to work in the round. Use a larger or smaller hook to obtain the gauge if necessary.

Hooks	Gauge per 4 x 4in (10 x 10cm)
4.25mm (G)	16 sc x 18 rnds
5mm (H)	15 sc x 17 rnds
5.5mm (I)	14 sc x 16 rnds

YARN

Medium weight yarn (weight 4) – **MC** is the main color and **CC** is a contrasting color (*see animal patterns for color suggestions*). The following charts indicate an estimated quantity of yarn needed for each pair of slippers, which is the combined amount of **MC** and **CC**. The weights given below are for Bernat Super Value yarn. If you are using a different yarn, you can calculate how much you need using the lengths table at the bottom of the page.

Type	Yarn amounts by weight for KIDS			Yarn amounts by weight for ADULTS		
	Small (S)	**Medium (M)**	**Large (L)**	**Small (S)**	**Medium (M)**	**Large (L)**
Shoes	2¼oz/ 65g	2½oz/ 75g	3oz/ 85g	3½oz/ 100g	3¾oz/ 105g	4¼oz/ 120g
Boots	3⅓oz/ 95g	3¾oz/ 105g	4oz/ 115g	5oz/ 140g	5½oz/ 160g	6½oz/ 180g
Slides	2oz/ 60g	2⅖oz/ 70g	2¾oz/ 80g	3½oz/ 95g	3¾oz/ 105g	4oz/ 115g

Type	Yarn amounts by length for KIDS			Yarn amounts by length for ADULTS		
	Small (S)	**Medium (M)**	**Large (L)**	**Small (S)**	**Medium (M)**	**Large (L)**
Shoes	140yds/ 128m	162yds/ 148m	184yds/ 168m	216yds/ 197m	238yds/ 217m	259yds/ 237m
Boots	205yds/ 188m	227yds/ 207m	248yds/ 227m	302yds/ 276m	346yds/ 316m	389yds/ 355m
Slides	130yds/ 118m	151yds/ 138m	173yds/ 158m	205yds/ 188m	227yds/ 207m	248yds/ 227m

Gussets

Make 2 (1 for each slipper). Work in rows using **MC** and a 4.25mm (G) hook.

KIDS - S (M, L)

To beg: Ch 8 (10, 12)

Row 1: (WS) Sc in second ch from hook (the skipped ch does not count as a st), sc in next 5 (7, 9) chs, 3 sc in last ch; working across the opposite side of the foundation ch, sc in next 6 (8, 10) chs; turn = 15 (19, 23) sts

Row 2: (RS) Ch 1 (does not count as a st), sc in first st, sc in next 5 (7, 9) sts, 2 sc in each of next 3 sts, sc in next 6 (8, 10) sts = 18 (22, 26) sts

Fasten off, leaving a 60in (153cm) tail for Slip Stitch joining or 20in (51cm) tail for Whipstitch and Mattress Stitch joining (*see Useful Information: Joining Gussets*).

ADULTS - S (M, L)

To beg: Ch 10 (12, 14)

Row 1: (RS) Sc in second ch from hook (the skipped ch does not count as a st), sc in next 7 (9, 11) chs, 3 sc in last ch; working across the opposite side of the foundation ch, sc in next 8 (10, 12) chs; turn = 19 (23, 27) sts

Row 2: (WS) Ch 1 (does not count as a st now and throughout), sc in first st, sc in next 7 (9, 11) sts, 2 sc in each of next 3 sts, sc in next 8 (10, 12) sts; turn = 22 (26, 30) sts

Row 3: (RS) Ch 1, sc in first st, sc in next 7 (9, 11) sts, 2 sc in next st, sc in next st, 2 sc in each of next 2 sts, sc in next st, 2 sc in next st, sc in next 8 (10, 12) sts = 26 (30, 34) sts

Fasten off, leaving a 75in (191cm) tail for Slip Stitch joining or 25in (64cm) tail for Whipstitch and Mattress Stitch joining (*see Useful Information: Joining Gussets*).

GUSSET Kids - S

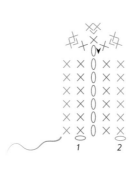

GUSSET Adults - S

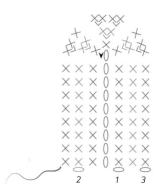

GUSSET Kids - M

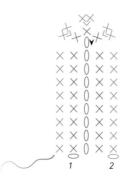

GUSSET Adults - M

GUSSET Kids - L

GUSSET Adults - L

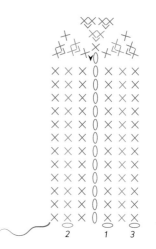

Double-Soles

Make 2 (1 for each slipper). Double-Soles are designed for stability, durability and comfort. To finish a double-sole, make 1 insole using **CC** and 1 outsole using **MC**, working both pieces in the same manner. If the main color is too light for outsoles, you can use **CC** and then change to **MC** after joining round. Work in the round with the following hooks:

Type	Hooks
Shoes	5mm (H)
Boots	5mm (H)
Slides	5.5mm (I)

NOTE:
Due to the stretchy texture of crochet fabric, there is no difference between the left and right slippers. Make both slippers in the same manner.

SOLE Kids – S

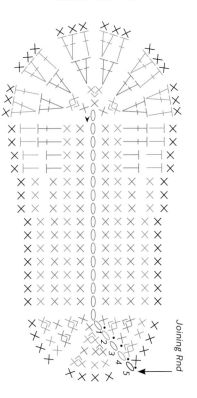

SOLE Kids – M

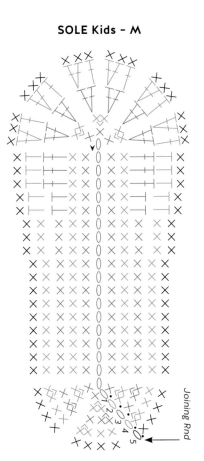

SOLE Kids – L

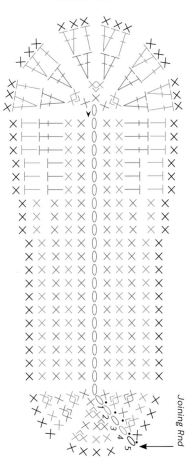

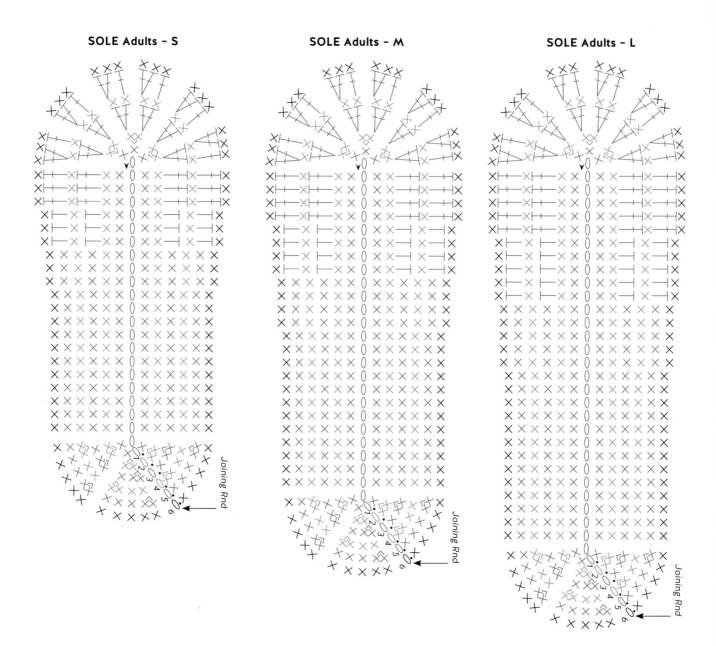

SOLE Adults – S   SOLE Adults – M   SOLE Adults – L

Joining Rnd

FINISHED MEASUREMENTS

These measurements are for the finished length of Double-Sole including joining round.

Type	Double-Sole Length for KIDS			Double-Sole Length for ADULTS		
	Small (S)	Medium (M)	Large (L)	Small (S)	Medium (M)	Large (L)
Shoes	6½in (16.5cm)	7¼in (18.5cm)	8in (20cm)	8½in (21.5cm)	9½in (24cm)	10½in (27cm)
Boots						
Slides	7in (18cm)	8in (20cm)	8¾in (22cm)	9¼in (23.5cm)	10¼in (26cm)	11½in (29cm)

KIDS - S (M, L)

To beg: Ch 17 (20, 23)

Rnd 1: Sc in second ch from hook (the skipped ch does not count as a st), sc in next 14 (17, 20) chs, 3 sc in last ch; working across the opposite side of the foundation ch, sc in next 14 (17, 20) chs, 2 sc in last ch; join = 34 (40, 46) sts

Rnd 2: Ch 1 (does not count as a st now and throughout), 2 sc in same st as join, sc in next 14 (17, 20) sts, 2 sc in each of next 3 sts, sc in next 14 (17, 20) sts, 2 sc in each of next 2 sts; join = 40 (46, 52) sts

Rnd 3: Ch 1, sc in same st as join, 2 sc in next st, sc in next 10 (12, 14) sts, hdc in next 2 (2, 3) sts, dc in next 2 (3, 3) sts, 2 dc in each of next 6 sts, dc in next 2 (3, 3) sts, hdc in next 2 (2, 3) sts, sc in next 10 (12, 14) sts, [sc in next st, 2 sc in next st] 2 times; join = 49 (55, 61) sts

Rnd 4: Ch 1, 2 sc in same st as join, sc in next 12 (14, 16) sts, hdc in next 4 (5, 6) sts, [dc in next st, 2 dc in next st] 6 times, hdc in each of next 4 (5, 6) sts, sc in next 10 (12, 14) sts, [2 sc in next st, sc in next 2 sts] 2 times; join = 58 (64, 70) sts

Fasten off and weave in ends.

ADULTS - S (M, L)

To beg: Ch 23 (27, 31)

Rnd 1: Sc in second ch from hook (the skipped ch does not count as a st), sc in next 20 (24, 28) chs, 3 sc in last ch; working across the opposite side of the foundation ch, sc in next 20 (24, 28) chs, 2 sc in last ch; join = 46 (54, 62) sts

Rnd 2: Ch 1 (does not count as a st now and throughout), 2 sc in same st as join, sc in next 20 (24, 28) sts, 2 sc in each of next 3 sts, sc in next 20 (24, 28) sts, 2 sc in each of next 2 sts; join = 52 (60, 68) sts

Rnd 3: Ch 1, sc in same st as join, 2 sc in next st, sc in next 14 (16, 18) sts, hdc in next 3 (4, 5) sts, dc in next 3 (4, 5) sts, 2 dc in each of next 6 sts, dc in next 3 (4, 5) sts, hdc in next 3 (4, 5) sts, sc in next 14 (16, 18) sts, [sc in next st, 2 sc in next st] 2 times; join = 61 (69, 77) sts

Rnd 4: Ch 1, 2 sc in same st as join, sc in next 54 (62, 70) sts, [2 sc in next st, sc in next 2 sts] 2 times; join = 64 (72, 80) sts

Rnd 5: Ch 1, sc in same st as join, sc in next 2 sts, 2 sc in next st, sc in next 14 (16, 18) sts, hdc in next 3 (4, 5) sts, dc in next 3 (4, 5) sts, [dc in next st, 2 dc in next st] 6 times, dc in next 3 (4, 5) sts, hdc in next 3 (4, 5) sts, sc in next 14 (16, 18) sts, [sc in next 3 sts, 2 sc in next st] 2 times; join = 73 (81, 89) sts

Fasten off and weave in ends.

JOINING SOLES

Line up the insole and outsole, holding them with WS facing each other, and with the outsole facing you **(fig 1)**.

Rnd	KIDS			ADULTS		
	Small (S)	**Medium (M)**	**Large (L)**	**Small (S)**	**Medium (M)**	**Large (L)**
Set-up	Mark 6 center stitches of the heel on the narrow side of the soles by placing the end markers through both layers; you should have 4 stitches between the markers **(figs 1 and 2)**			Mark 7 center stitches of the heel on the narrow side of the soles by placing the end markers through both layers; you should have 5 stitches between the markers **(figs 1 and 2)**		
	With the outsole facing you, join **MC** in stitch with marker on the left **(fig 3)**, or marker on the right for left-handed crochet (*see Useful Information: Left-Handed Crochet*). Using the same hook as for the soles, work the joining round through the stitches of both pieces at the same time, removing markers as you go **(fig 4)**					
Joining (RS)	Ch 1 (does not count as a st), sc in same st as join, sc in each st around; join = 58 (64, 70) sts			Ch 1 (does not count as a st), sc in same st as join, sc in each st around; join = 73 (81, 89) sts		

Do not fasten off and do not turn. Continue to work the upper of your slippers with **MC**, keeping the outsole as the RS and insole as the WS (*see Upper of Shoes and Boots / Upper of Slides*).

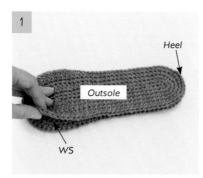

Center sts of the heel on narrow side of the soles

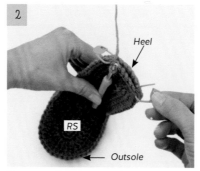

Center sts between markers:
4 sts for Kids - S, M, L
5 sts for Adults - S, M, L

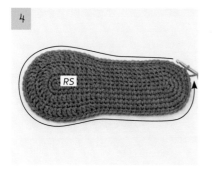

MAKING SLIPPERS

Upper of Shoes and Boots

With the outsole facing you, begin by working around the joining round of the sole, using **MC** and a 4.25mm (G) hook.

KIDS – S (M, L)

Work around 58 (64, 70) sts of the joining round:

Rnd 1: Ch 2 (does not count as a st), dc in same st as join, dc in each st around; join = 58 (64, 70) sts

Rnds 2 – 3: Ch 1 (does not count as a st now and throughout), fpdc around st with join, bpdc around next st, [fpdc around next st, bpdc around next st] 28 (31, 34) times; join = 58 (64, 70) sts

Rnd 4: Ch 1, [fpdc around next fpdc, bpdc around next bpdc] 5 (6, 7) times, sc in next 8 (9, 10) sts, [sc in next st, sc2tog] 6 times, sc in next 8 (9, 10) sts, [fpdc around next fpdc, bpdc around next bpdc] 7 (8, 9) times; join = 52 (58, 64) sts

Rnd 5: Ch 1, [fpdc around next fpdc, bpdc around next bpdc] 4 (5, 6) times, sc in next 5 (4, 3) sts and place **Marker A** in last st made, sc in next 5 (7, 9) sts, [sc2tog 6 times, sc in next 6 (8, 10) sts and place **Marker B** in last st made, sc in next 4 (3, 2) sts, [fpdc around next fpdc, bpdc around next bpdc] 6 (7, 8) times; join = 46 (52, 58) sts

Do not fasten off, but leave the last loop on the hook while assembling the gusset (*see Assembling Gusset*).

ADULTS – S (M, L)

Work around 73 (81, 89) sts of the joining round:

Rnd 1: Ch 2 (does not count as a st), dc in same st as join, dc in each st to last 2 sts, dc2tog; join = 72 (80, 88) sts

Rnds 2 – 3: Ch 1 (does not count as a st now and throughout), fpdc around st with join, bpdc around next st, [fpdc around next st, bpdc around next st] 35 (39, 43) times; join = 72 (80, 88) sts

Rnd 4: Ch 1, [fpdc around next fpdc, bpdc around next bpdc] 7 (8, 9) times, sc in next 40 (44, 48) sts, [fpdc around next fpdc, bpdc around next bpdc] 9 (10, 11) times; join = 72 (80, 88) sts

Rnd 5: Ch 1, [fpdc around next fpdc, bpdc around next bpdc] 6 (7, 8) times, sc in next 13 (15, 17) sts, [sc in next st, sc2tog] 6 times, sc in next 13 (15, 17) sts, [fpdc around next fpdc, bpdc around next bpdc] 8 (9, 10) times; join = 66 (74, 82) sts

Rnd 6: Ch 1, [fpdc around next fpdc, bpdc around next bpdc] 5 (6, 7) times, sc in next 6 sts and place **Marker A** in last st made, sc in next 9 (11, 13) sts, [sc2tog 6 times, sc in next 10 (12, 14) sts and place **Marker B** in last st made, sc in next 5 sts, [fpdc around next fpdc, bpdc around next bpdc] 7 (8, 9) times; join = 60 (68, 76) sts

Do not fasten off, but leave the last loop on the hook while assembling the gusset (*see Assembling Gusset*).

ASSEMBLING GUSSET

Place the gusset in space between markers. The marked stitches should be straight across from each other, indicating the first and last stitches of the gusset **(fig 1)**. Using the long tail from the gusset, join the edges from **Marker A** to **Marker B (fig 2)**, following the joining method you prefer (*see Useful Information: Joining Gussets*). Joining the gussets precisely is crucial for a good finish so follow each step carefully.

Fasten off and weave in the end, but do not remove the markers yet. Pick up your yarn and hook from the last working round and continue to work around the edge **(fig 3)**.

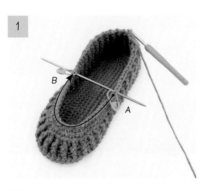

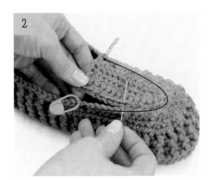

EDGING

NOTE:

The beginning Ch 1 does not count as a st throughout. Therefore, do not skip the first st with join.

Rnd	KIDS			ADULTS		
	Small (S)	**Medium (M)**	**Large (L)**	**Small (S)**	**Medium (M)**	**Large (L)**
1	Ch 1, sc in each st to **Marker A**, skip st with marker, 5 sc evenly across the gusset to **Marker B**, skip st with marker, sc in each st to beg st; join and remove markers = 33 (35, 37) sts			Ch 1, sc in each st to **Marker A**, skip st with marker, 7 sc evenly across the gusset to **Marker B**, skip st with marker, sc in each st to beg st; join and remove markers = 41 (45, 49) sts		
2	Ch 1, [sc in next 3 sts, sc2tog] 6 times, sc in next st, sc2tog; join = 26 sts	Ch 1, [sc in next 3 sts, sc2tog] 7 times; join = 28 sts	Ch 1, [sc in next 3 sts, sc2tog] 7 times, sc in next 2 sts; join = 30 sts	Ch 1, [sc in next 3 sts, sc2tog] 7 times, [sc in next st, sc2tog] 2 times; join = 32 sts	Ch 1, [sc in next 3 sts, sc2tog] 9 times; join = 36 sts	Ch 1, [sc in next 3 sts, sc2tog] 9 times, sc in next 4 sts; join = 40 sts
3	Ch 1, sc in each st around; join = 26 (28, 30) sts			Ch 1, sc in each st around; join = 32 (36, 40) sts		

Fasten off and weave in the ends for Shoes or continue to work Ankle Cuffs for Boots. Finish soles with a non-slip lining if desired (*see Non-Slip Soles*).

ANKLE CUFFS

NOTE:

The beginning Ch 2 in Rnd 1 does not count as a st. Therefore, do not skip the first st with join.

Rnd	KIDS			ADULTS		
	Small (S)	**Medium (M)**	**Large (L)**	**Small (S)**	**Medium (M)**	**Large (L)**
1	Ch 2, [dc in next 3 sts, 2 dc in next st, dc in next 2 sts, 2 dc in next st] 3 times, dc in next 2 sts, 2 dc in next st, dc in next st, 2 dc in next st; join = 34 sts	Ch 2, [dc in next 3 sts, 2 dc in next st] 6 times, [dc in next st, 2 dc in next st] 2 times; join = 36 sts	Ch 2, [dc in next 3 sts, 2 dc in next st] 7 times, dc in next st, 2 dc in next st; join = 38 sts	Ch 2, [dc in next 3 sts, 2 dc in next st] 8 times; join = 40 sts	Ch 2, [dc in next 4 sts, 2 dc in next st, dc in next 3 sts, 2 dc in next st] 4 times; join = 44 sts	Ch 2, [dc in next 4 sts, 2 dc in next st] 8 times; join = 48 st
2	Ch 1 (does not count as a st), fpdc around st with join, bpdc around next st; [fpdc around next st, bpdc around next st] repeat around; join = 34 (36, 38)			Ch 1 (does not count as a st), fpdc around st with join, bpdc around next st; [fpdc around next st, bpdc around next st] repeat around; join = 40 (44, 48)		
Next	Repeat Rnd 2 another 4 times	Repeat Rnd 2 another 5 times	Repeat Rnd 2 another 6 times	Repeat Rnd 2 another 7 times	Repeat Rnd 2 another 8 times	Repeat Rnd 2 another 9 times

Fasten off and weave in the ends. Fold the cuff down or keep it straight up when wearing. Finish soles with a non-slip lining if desired (*see Non-Slip Soles*).

MAKING SLIPPERS

Upper of Slides

With the outsole facing you, begin by working around the joining round of the sole, using **MC** and a 5mm (H) hook.

KIDS – S (M, L)

Work around 58 (64, 70) sts of the joining round:

Rnd 1: Ch 1 (does not count as a st now and throughout), sc in same st as join, sc in next 4 (5, 6) sts, hdc in next 5 (6, 7) sts, dc in next 34 (36, 38) sts, hdc in next 5 (6, 7) sts, sc in next 9 (10, 11) sts; join = 58 (64, 70) sts

Rnd 2: Ch 1, sc in same st as join, sc in next 9 (11, 13) sts; [fpdc around next dc, bpdc around next dc] 17 (18, 19) times, sc in next 14 (16, 18) sts; join = 58 (64, 70) sts

Continue working in rows from now on, using a stitch marker to indicate the beginning of short rows (**Beg Marker**). Remove this marker at the end of the following row.

Row 3: (RS) Skip st with join, sl st in next 4 (5, 6) sts (do not count as sts), sc in next st and place **Beg Marker** in st just made, sc in next 4 (5, 6) sts; [fpdc around next fpdc, bpdc around next bpdc] 17 (18, 19) times, sc in next 5 (6, 7) sts; turn, leaving the remaining sts unworked for heel = 44 (48, 52) sts

Row 4: (WS) Skip first st, sl st in next 2 sts (do not count as sts), sc in next st and place **Beg Marker** in st just made, sc in next 9 (11, 13) sts, [sc in next st, sc2tog] 6 times, sc in next 10 (12, 14) sts; turn, leaving the remaining 3 sts unworked = 32 (36, 40) sts

Row 5: (RS) Skip first st, sl st in next 2 sts (do not count as sts), sc in next st and place **Beg Marker** in st just made, sc in next 25 (29, 33) sts; turn, leaving the remaining 3 sts unworked = 26 (30, 34) sts

Row 6: (WS) Ch 1, sc in first st and place **Marker B** in st just made, sc in next 4 (6, 8) sts, [sc2tog] 8 times, sc in next 5 (7, 9) sts and place **Marker A** in last st made; turn = 18 (22, 26) sts

Do not fasten off, but leave the last loop on the hook while assembling the gusset.

ADULTS – S (M, L)

Work around 73 (81, 89) sts of the joining round:

Rnd 1: Ch 1 (does not count as a st now and throughout), sc in same st as join, sc in next 6 (7, 8) sts, hdc in next 7 (8, 9) sts, dc in next 40 (44, 48) sts, hdc in next 7 (8, 9) sts, sc in next 12 (13, 14) sts; join = 73 (81, 89) sts

Rnd 2: Ch 1, sc in same st as join, sc in next 13 (15, 17) sts, [fpdc around next dc, bpdc around next dc] 20 (22, 24) times, sc in next 19 (21, 23) sts; join = 73 (81, 89) sts

Continue working in rows from now on, using a stitch marker to indicate the beginning of short rows (**Beg Marker**). Remove this marker at the end of the following row.

Row 3: (RS) Skip st with join, sl st in next 6 (7, 8) sts (do not count as sts), sc in next st and place **Beg Marker** in st just made, sc in next 6 (7, 8) sts, [fpdc around next fpdc, bpdc around next bpdc] 20 (22, 24) times, sc in next 7 (8, 9) sts; turn, leaving the remaining sts unworked for heel = 54 (60, 66) sts

Row 4: (WS) Skip first st, sl st in next 2 sts (do not count as sts), sc in next st and place **Beg Marker** in st just made, sc in next 47 (53, 59) sts; turn, leaving the last 3 sts unworked = 48 (54, 60) sts

Row 5: (RS) Skip first st, sl st in next 2 sts (do not count as sts), sc in next st and place **Beg Marker** in st just made, sc in next 11 (14, 17) sts, [sc in next st, sc2tog] 6 times, sc in next 12 (15, 18) sts; turn, leaving the last 3 sts unworked = 36 (42, 48) sts

Row 6: (WS) Skip first st, sl st in next 2 sts (do not count as sts), sc in next st and place **Beg Marker** in st just made, sc in next 29 (35, 41) sts; turn, leaving the last 3 sts unworked = 30 (36, 42) sts

Row 7: (RS) Ch 1, sc in first st and place **Marker A** in st just made, sc in next 10 (11, 12) sts, [sc2tog] 4 (6, 8) times, sc in next 11 (12, 13) sts and place **Marker B** in last st made; do not turn = 26 (30, 34) sts

Do not fasten off, but leave the last loop on the hook while assembling the gusset.

ASSEMBLING GUSSET

Place the gusset in space between markers. The marked stitches indicate the first and last stitches of the gusset. Using the long tail from the gusset, join the edges from **Marker A** to **Marker B** **(figs 1 and 2)**, following the joining method you prefer (see *Useful Information: Joining Gussets*). Joining the gussets precisely is crucial for a good finish so follow each step carefully. Fasten off and weave in the end.

EDGING

Pick up your yarn and hook from the last working round and continue to work around the raw edge of slides: With RS facing you, work sc evenly around entire edge, removing markers as you go **(fig 3)**, sl st in beg st. Fasten off and weave in the end. Finish soles with a non-slip lining if desired (see *Non-Slip Soles*).

Non-Slip Soles

Slippers made of yarn may become slippery on an uncarpeted floor. For safety, you can add non-slip patches to the soles of your slippers using a regular gripped shelf liner.

Trace the non-slip sole template onto a piece of transparent paper and cut it out. Use this template for cutting 2 gripped patches from a shelf liner.

Place the gripped patches on your crochet soles, positioning them evenly from the center out, as the patches are slightly smaller than the soles. Thread the needle with **MC** and sew a running stitch across the center, then turn and stitch again on each side of your center line **(figs 4 and 5)**.

Using the same yarn, whipstitch around the edge of the patches **(fig 6)**. Fasten off and weave in the end.

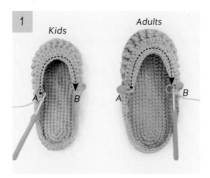

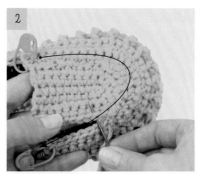

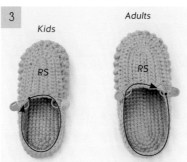

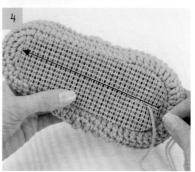

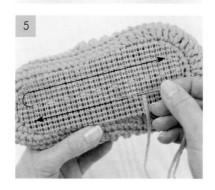

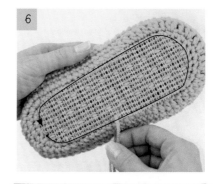

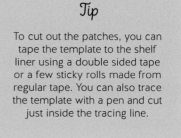

Tip

To cut out the patches, you can tape the template to the shelf liner using a double sided tape or a few sticky rolls made from regular tape. You can also trace the template with a pen and cut just inside the tracing line.

NON-SLIP SOLE
TEMPLATES
(actual size)

You can download printable versions of these templates from: www.davidandcharles.com

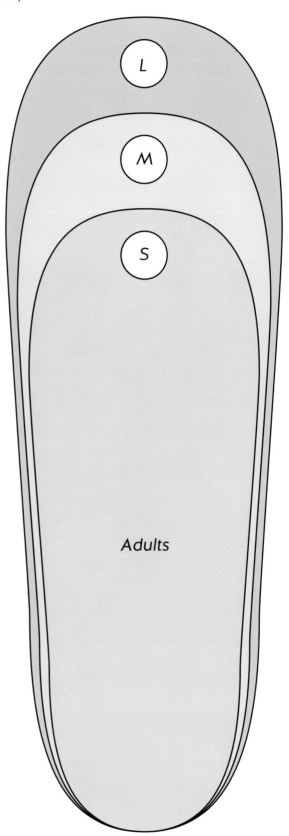

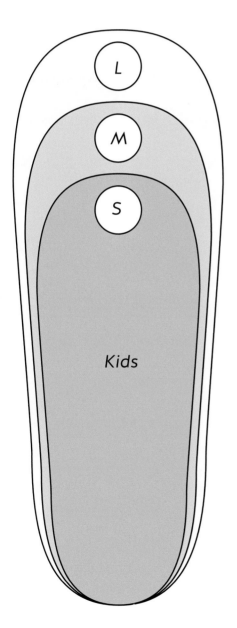

The Slippers

the Snuggly Pug

- - - - - - - -

The snuggly pugs will fit "pugfectly" on your feet. They don't bark or bite, but will protect your toes from getting cold.

Materials

YARN - WEIGHT 4

A small amount of **CC1** (Chocolate) for ears and muzzle, **CC2** (Black) for nose.

Use **MC** (Warm Brown) for the upper of your slippers and outsoles, and use **CC2** (Black) for insoles.

HOOKS

3.5mm (E), 3.75mm (F), 4.25mm (G)

ADDITIONAL MATERIALS

- Buttons for eyes: 4 x 15mm for Kids S (M, L) or 4 x 20mm for Adults S (M, L)
- White felt for highlighting eyes
- Stitch marker
- Sewing needle and thread
- Tapestry needle and scissors

STITCH SUMMARY

Ch, sl st, sc, magic ring (optional), join

SKILLS

Working in rows and in the round, working across the opposite side of the foundation chain, increasing, sewing

Skill Level

Muzzle

Make 1 for each slipper. Work in the round with **CC1** and a 4.25mm (G) hook.

KIDS – S, M, L

To beg: Ch 3, sl st in third ch from hook to form a ring (or start with a magic ring)

Rnd 1: Ch 1 (does not count as a st now and throughout), 6 sc in ring; join = 6 sts

Rnd 2: Ch 1, sc in st with join, 3 sc in next st, [sc in next st, 3 sc in next st] 2 times; join = 12 sts

Rnd 3: Ch 1, sc in same st as join, sc in next st, 3 sc in next st, [sc in next 3 sts, 3 sc in next st] 2 times, sc in last st; join = 18 sts

Rnd 4: Ch 1, sc in same st as join, sc in next 2 sts, 3 sc in next st, sc in next 4 sts, 2 sc in next st, sc in next st and place **Marker** in st just made to indicate the top of the muzzle, 2 sc in next st, sc in next 4 sts, 3 sc in next st, sc in next 2 sts; join = 24 sts

Fasten off, leaving a long tail for sewing.

ADULTS – S, M, L

To beg: Ch 3, sl st in third ch from hook to form a ring (or start with a magic ring)

Rnds 1 – 3: Same as for Kids

Rnd 4: Ch 1, sc in same st as join, sc in next 2 sts, 3 sc in next st, [sc in next 5 sts, 3 sc in next st] 2 times, sc in next 2 sts; join = 24 sts

Rnd 5: Ch 1, sc in same st as join, sc in next 3 sts, 3 sc in next st, sc in next 6 sts, 2 sc in next st, sc in next st and place **Marker** in st just made to indicate the top of the muzzle, 2 sc in next st, sc in next 6 sts, 3 sc in next st, sc in next 3 sts; join = 30 sts

Fasten off, leaving a long tail for sewing.

Nose

Make 1 for each slipper. Work in the round with **CC2**, using a 3.5mm (E) hook for Kids' sizes or 3.75mm (F) hook for Adults' sizes.

To beg: Ch 4

Rnd 1: Sc in second ch from hook (the skipped ch does not count as a st), sc in next ch, 3 sc in last ch; working across the opposite side of the foundation ch, sc in next ch, 2 sc in last ch; join = 8 sts

Fasten off, leaving a long tail for sewing.

MUZZLE
Kids – S, M, L

Marker

MUZZLE
Adults – S, M, L

Marker

NOSE
All Sizes

EAR
Kids – S, M, L

EAR
Adults – S, M, L

Ears

Make 2 for each slipper.
Work in rows with **CC1** and a
4.25mm (G) hook.

KIDS – S, M, L

To beg: Ch 6

Row 1: (WS) Sc in second ch from
hook (the skipped ch does not
count as a st), sc in next 3 chs,
3 sc in last ch; working across the
opposite side of the foundation ch,
sc in next 4 chs; turn = 11 sts

Row 2: (RS) Ch 1 (does not count
as a st), sc in first st, sc in next
4 sts, 3 sc in next st, sc in next 5 sts
= 13 sts

Fasten off, leaving a long tail
for sewing.

ADULTS – S, M, L

To beg: Ch 7

Row 1: (RS) Sc in second ch from
hook (the skipped ch does not
count as a st), sc in next 4 chs,
3 sc in last ch; working across the
opposite side of the foundation ch,
sc in next 5 chs; turn = 13 sts

Row 2: (WS) Ch 1 (does not count
as a st now and throughout), sc in
first st, sc in next 5 sts, 3 sc in next
st, sc in next 6 sts; turn = 15 sts

Row 3: (RS) Ch 1, sc in first st, sc in
next 6 sts, 3 sc in next st, sc in next
7 sts = 17 sts

Fasten off, leaving a long tail
for sewing.

Finishing Slippers

With the marker facing up, position
the muzzle on the front of the
slipper. Remove the marker and
backstitch around onto the slipper
using the long **CC1** tail **(fig 1)**.
Fasten off and weave in the end.

Position the nose by the top edge
of the muzzle and backstitch
around onto the muzzle using the
long **CC2** tail **(fig 2)**. Fasten off and
weave in the end.

To finish the eyes, use 15mm
buttons for Kids' sizes or 20mm
buttons for Adults' sizes. Sew
the buttons on each side of the
muzzle, adding a small white
felt circle as a highlighting layer
under each button (see *Useful
Information: Sewing Buttons*).

Using the gusset seams as guides,
position the ears on each side of
the gusset **(fig 3)**.

Sew the ears on with whipstitch
using the long **CC1** tail from each
ear **(fig 4)**. Fasten off and weave in
the ends.

the Cuddly Bear

· · · · · · · · · · · · · · ·

This is one type of bear that you do not need to back away from. With these cuddly bears on your feet, find a warm blanket and hibernate for a bit.

Materials

YARN - WEIGHT 4

A small amount of **MC** (Warm Brown) for outer ears, **CC1** (Beige) for inner ears and muzzle, **CC2** (Chocolate) for nose.

Use **MC** (Warm Brown) for the upper of your slippers and outsoles, and use any contrasting color for insoles.

HOOKS

3.5mm (E), 3.75mm (F), 4.25mm (G)

ADDITIONAL MATERIALS

· Stitch marker
· Buttons for eyes: 4 x 15mm for Kids S (M, L) or 4 x 20mm for Adults S (M, L)
· Sewing needle and thread
· Tapestry needle and scissors

STITCH SUMMARY

Ch, sl st, sc, magic ring (optional), join

SKILLS

Working in rows and in the round, working across the opposite side of the foundation chain, increasing, sewing

Skill Level

● ○ ○ ○

Muzzle

Make 1 for each slipper. Work in spiral rounds with **CC1** and a 4.25mm (G) hook. Use a stitch marker to mark the start of each round as you go.

KIDS – S, M, L

To beg: Ch 3, sl st in third ch from hook to form a ring (or start with a magic ring)

Rnd 1: Ch 1 (does not count as a st), 6 sc in ring; do not join now and throughout = 6 sts

Rnd 2: 2 sc in first st of previous rnd, 2 sc in each of next 5 sts = 12 sts

Rnd 3: 2 sc in each st around = 24 sts

Rnd 4: Sc in each st around = 24 sts

Sl st in next st and fasten off, leaving a long tail for sewing.

ADULTS – S, M, L

To beg: Ch 3, sl st in third ch from hook to form a ring (or start with a magic ring)

Rnds 1 – 4: Same as for Kids

Rnd 5: [Sc in next st, 2 sc in next st] 12 times = 36 sts

Sl st in next st and fasten off, leaving a long tail for sewing.

Nose

Make 1 for each slipper. Work in the round with **CC2**, using a 3.5mm (E) hook for Kids' sizes or 3.75mm (F) hook for Adults' sizes.

To beg: Ch 4

Rnd 1: Sc in second ch from hook (the skipped ch does not count as a st), sc in next ch, 3 sc in last ch; working across the opposite side of the foundation ch, sc in next ch, 2 sc in last ch; join = 8 sts

Fasten off, leaving a long tail for sewing.

Ears

Make 2 for each slipper. Work in rows with a 4.25mm (G) hook.

KIDS – S, M, L

INNER EAR:
For each ear, make 1 inner ear using **CC1**.

To beg: Ch 3, sl st in third ch from hook to form a ring (or start with a magic ring)

Row 1: Ch 1 (does not count as a st now and throughout), 4 sc in ring; turn = 4 sts

Row 2: Ch 1, 2 sc in first st, 2 sc in each of next 3 sts = 8 sts

Fasten off and weave in the ends.

OUTER EAR:
For each ear, make 1 outer ear using **MC**. Work same as inner ear but do not fasten off. Turn and proceed to joining row.

MUZZLE
Kids – S, M, L

MUZZLE
Adults – S, M, L

EAR
Kids – S, M, L

Inner Ear

Outer Ear

Joining Row

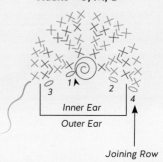

EAR
Adults – S, M, L

Inner Ear

Outer Ear

Joining Row

NOSE
All Sizes

JOINING ROW:

Place the inner ear on top of the outer ear with WS facing each other and work the next row through both pieces at the same time, using the working yarn from the outer ear.

Row 3: (RS) Ch 1, 2 sc in first st, sc in next st, [2 sc in next st, sc in next st] 3 times = 12 sts

Fasten off, leaving a long tail for sewing.

ADULTS – S, M, L

INNER EAR:

For each ear, make 1 inner ear using **CC1**.

To beg: Ch 3, sl st in third ch from hook to form a ring (or start with a magic ring)

Rows 1 – 2: Same as for Kids; turn

Row 3: Ch 1, 2 sc in first st, sc in next st; [2 sc in next st, sc in next st] 3 times = 12 sts

Fasten off and weave in the ends.

OUTER EAR:

For each ear, make 1 outer ear using **MC**. Work same as inner ear but do not fasten off. Turn and proceed to joining row.

JOINING ROW:

Place the inner ear on top of the outer ear with WS facing each other and work the next row through both pieces at the same time, using the working yarn from the outer ear.

Row 4: (RS) Ch 1, 2 sc in first st, sc in next 2 sts, [2 sc in next st, sc in next 2 sts] 3 times = 16 sts

Fasten off, leaving a long tail for sewing.

Finishing Slippers

Position the muzzle on the front of the slipper and backstitch around onto the slipper using the long **CC1** tail **(fig 1)**. Fasten off and weave in the end.

Position the nose by the top edge of the muzzle and backstitch around onto the muzzle using the long **CC2** tail, then make a straight stitch from the center of the nose down **(fig 2)**. Fasten off and weave in the end.

To finish the eyes, use 15mm buttons for Kids' sizes or 20mm buttons for Adults' sizes. Sew the buttons on each side of the gusset seams, placing them right up against the muzzle (see *Useful Information: Sewing Buttons*).

Using the gusset seams as guides, position the ears on each side of the gusset **(fig 3)**.

Whipstitch the ears around the bottom edge onto the slipper, using the long **MC** tail from each ear **(fig 4)**. Fasten off and weave in the ends.

Gusset

the Happy Penguin

Slide into the huddle with these adorable penguin slippers. They will keep your feet warm, your heart happy and are something the whole family can enjoy.

Materials

YARN - WEIGHT 4

A small amount of **MC** (Black) for wings, **CC1** (White) for face, **CC2** (Yellow) for beak.

Use **MC** (Black) for the upper of your slippers and outsoles, and use **CC1** (White) for insoles.

HOOKS

3.75mm (F), 4.25mm (G)

ADDITIONAL MATERIALS

- Stitch marker
- Buttons for eyes: 4 x 10mm for Kids S (M, L) or 4 x 15mm for Adults S (M, L)
- Sewing needle and thread
- Tapestry needle and scissors

STITCH SUMMARY

Ch, sl st, sc, magic ring (optional), join

SKILLS

Working in rows and in the round, increasing, sewing

Skill Level

Face

Make 1 for each slipper. To finish each face, make 2 circles and sew them together. Work in spiral rounds with **CC1** and a 4.25mm (G) hook. Use a stitch marker to mark the start of each round as you go.

KIDS – S, M, L

To beg: Ch 3, sl st in third ch from hook to form a ring (or start with a magic ring)

Rnd 1: Ch 1 (does not count as a st), 6 sc in ring; do not join now and throughout = 6 sts

Rnd 2: 2 sc in first st of previous rnd, 2 sc in each of next 5 sts = 12 sts

Rnd 3: [Sc in next st, 2 sc in next st] 6 times = 18 sts

Sl st in next st and fasten off, leaving a long tail for sewing when finishing the first circle and weaving in the end of the second circle.

ADULTS – S, M, L

To beg: Ch 3, sl st in third ch from hook to form a ring (or start with a magic ring)

Rnds 1 – 2: Same as for Kids

Rnd 3: 2 sc in each st around = 24 sts

Rnd 4: Sc in each st around = 24 sts

Sl st in next st and fasten off, leaving a long tail for sewing when finishing the first circle and weaving in the end of the second circle.

Finishing Face

Place 2 circles side by side and whipstitch across 3 sts using the long **CC1** tail from the first circle **(fig 1)**. Do not fasten off, but keep the long tail for future assembling.

To finish eyes, use 10mm buttons for Kids' sizes or 15mm buttons for Adults' sizes. Sew 1 button in the center of each circle (*see Useful Information: Sewing Buttons*).

Beak

Make 1 for each slipper. Work in rows with **CC2** and a 3.75mm (F) hook.

KIDS – S, M, L

To beg: Ch 2

Row 1: (WS) 3 sc in second ch from hook (the skipped ch does not count as a st); turn = 3 sts

Row 2: (RS) Ch 1 (does not count as a st), 2 sc in first st, 3 sc in next st, 2 sc in last st = 7 sts

Fasten off, leaving a long tail for sewing.

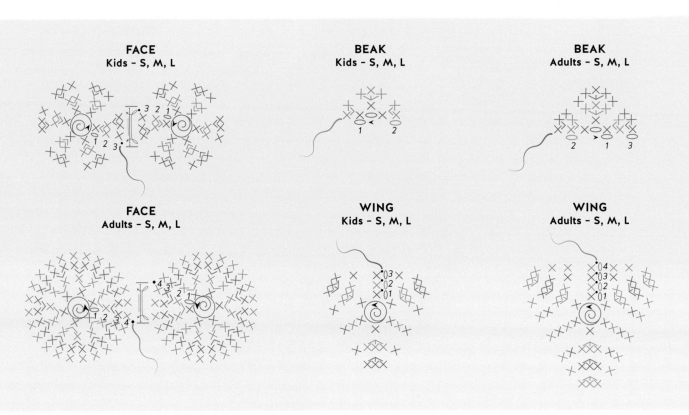

FACE
Kids - S, M, L

BEAK
Kids - S, M, L

BEAK
Adults - S, M, L

FACE
Adults - S, M, L

WING
Kids - S, M, L

WING
Adults - S, M, L

ADULTS – S, M, L

To beg: Ch 2

Row 1: (RS) 3 sc in second ch from hook (the skipped ch does not count as a st); turn = 3 sts

Row 2: (WS) Ch 1 (does not count as a st now and throughout), 2 sc in first st, 3 sc in next st, 2 sc in last st; turn = 7 sts

Row 3: (RS) Ch 1, 2 sc in first st, sc in next 2 sts, 3 sc in next st, sc in next 2 sts, 2 sc in last st = 11 sts

Fasten off, leaving a long tail for sewing.

Wings

Make 2 for each slipper. Work in the round with **MC** and a 4.25mm (G) hook.

KIDS – S, M, L

To beg: Ch 3, sl st in third ch from hook to form a ring (or start with a magic ring)

Rnd 1: Ch 1 (does not count as a st now and throughout), 6 sc in ring; join = 6 sts

Rnd 2: Ch 1, sc in same st as join, 3 sc in next st, [sc in next st, 3 sc in next st] 2 times; join = 12 sts

Rnd 3: Ch 1, sc in same st as join, sc in next st, 3 sc in next st, [sc in next 3 sts, 3 sc in next st] 2 times, sc in last st; join = 18 sts

Fasten off, leaving a long tail for sewing.

ADULTS – S, M, L

To beg: Ch 3, sl st in third ch from hook to form a ring (or start with a magic ring)

Rnds 1 – 3: Same as for Kids

Rnd 4: Ch 1, sc in same st as join, sc in next 2 sts, 3 sc in next st, [sc in next 5 sts, 3 sc in next st] 2 times, sc in next 2 sts; join = 24 sts

Fasten off, leaving a long tail for sewing.

Finishing Slippers

Position the face on the front of the slipper and backstitch around onto the slipper using the long **CC1** tail **(fig 2)**. Fasten off and weave in the end.

Position the beak in the center of the face below the eyes, facing it towards the foot opening. Using the long **CC2** tail from the beak, whipstitch across the top edge and backstitch the sides of the beak to the face, bringing the needle from one side to the other through the stitches marked with a dashed line **(fig 3)**. Leave the bottom corner unstitched. Fasten off and weave in the end.

Position the wings on each side of the slipper below the face. Bring the long **MC** tail through the stitches of the first wing to the closest corner and whipstitch across the top edge **(fig 4)**. Fasten off and weave in the end. Sew the second wing in the same manner.

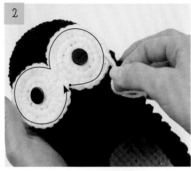

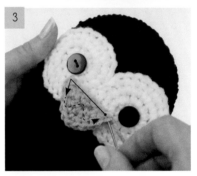

Tip

For a different look, you can omit wings and sew the beak, facing it towards the toes.

the Zingy Dinosaur

- - - - - - - -

All dinosaur fans will feel fierce while wearing these zingy triceratops slippers. Staying at home is fun and enjoyable if you have prehistoric dinosaur friends who look after your feet and toes, keeping them warm.

Materials

YARN - WEIGHT 4

A small amount of **MC** (Lush Green) for frill, **CC1** (Yellow) for spikes, **CC2** (Beige) for muzzle, **CC3** (White) for horns.

Use **MC** (Lush Green) for the upper of your slippers and outsoles, and use **CC1** (Yellow) for insoles.

HOOK

4.25mm (G)

ADDITIONAL MATERIALS

- Buttons for eyes: 4 x 15mm for Kids S (M, L) or 4 x 20mm for Adults S (M, L)
- Sewing needle and thread
- Tapestry needle and scissors

STITCH SUMMARY

Ch, sl st, sc, hdc, dc, fpdc, bpdc, sc2tog, sc3tog, PC, join

SKILLS

Working in rows and in the round, working across the opposite side of the foundation chain, increasing, decreasing, sewing

Skill Level

●●●○

Muzzle

Make 1 for each slipper. Work in the round with **CC2** and a 4.25mm (G) hook.

KIDS – S, M, L

To beg: Ch 10

Rnd 1: Sc in second ch from hook (the skipped ch does not count as a st), sc in next 7 chs, 3 sc in last ch; working across the opposite side of the foundation ch, sc in next 7 chs, 2 sc in last ch; join = 20 sts

Rnd 2: Ch 1 (does not count as a st), 2 sc in same st as join, sc in next 3 sts, 3 sc in next st, sc in next 3 sts, 2 sc in each of next 3 sts, sc in next 2 sts, sc3tog, sc in next 2 sts, 2 sc in each of next 2 sts; join = 26 sts

Fasten off, leaving a long tail for sewing.

ADULTS – S, M, L

To beg: Ch 12

Rnd 1: Sc in second ch from hook (the skipped ch does not count as a st), sc in next 9 chs, 3 sc in last ch; working across the opposite side of the foundation ch, sc in next 9 chs, 2 sc in last ch; join = 24 sts

Rnd 2: Ch 1 (does not count as a st), 2 sc in same st as join, sc in next 4 sts, 3 sc in next st, sc in next 4 sts, 2 sc in each of next 3 sts, sc in next 3 sts, sc3tog, sc in next 3 sts, 2 sc in each of next 2 sts; join = 30 sts

Fasten off, leaving a long tail for sewing.

Horns

Make 3 for each slipper. Work in rows with **CC3** and a 4.25mm (G) hook.

KIDS – S, M, L

To beg: Ch 6

Row 1: (RS) Sl st in second ch from hook (the skipped ch does not count as a st), sc in next ch, hdc in next 2 chs, dc in last ch = 5 sts

Fasten off, leaving a long tail for sewing.

ADULTS – S, M, L

To beg: Ch 7

Row 1: (RS) Sl st in second ch from hook (the skipped ch does not count as a st), sc in next ch, hdc in next 2 chs, dc in next 2 chs = 6 sts

Fasten off, leaving a long tail for sewing.

MUZZLE
Kids – S, M, L

MUZZLE
Adults – S, M, L

Frill

Make 1 for each slipper.
Work in rows with **MC** and a
4.25mm (G) hook.

KIDS – S, M, L

To beg: Leaving a long tail at the beginning for sewing, ch 19

Row 1: (WS) Sc in second ch from hook (the skipped ch does not count as a st), sc in each ch across; turn = 18 sts

Row 2: (RS) Ch 2 (counts as dc now and throughout), dc in first st, [dc in next st, 2 dc in next st] 8 times, dc in last st; turn = 27 sts

Row 3: (WS) Ch 2, skip first st, [bpdc around next st, fpdc around next st] 12 times, bpdc around next st, dc in last st, changing to **CC1**; turn without breaking off **MC** = 27 sts

Row 4: (RS) With **CC1**, ch 1 (does not count as a st now and throughout), sc in first st, PC in next st, [sc in next 3 sts, PC in next st] 6 times, sc in last st; turn = 7 PC and 20 sc

Row 5: (WS) Ch 1, sc in first st, sc in each st across, changing to **MC** at the end of the row; break off **CC1** and turn = 27 sts

Row 6: (RS) With **MC**, ch 2, skip first st, dc in next 26 sts, turn = 27 sts

Row 7: (WS) Same as Row 3

Row 8: (RS) Ch 1, sc in first st, sc2tog, [sc in next st, sc2tog] 8 times = 18 sts

Fasten off, leaving a long tail for sewing.

ADULTS – S, M, L

To beg: Leaving a long tail at the beginning for sewing, ch 22

Row 1: (RS) Sc in second ch from hook (the skipped ch does not count as a st), sc in each ch across; turn = 21 sts

Row 2: (WS) Ch 2 (counts as dc now and throughout), skip first st, [2 dc in next st, dc in next st] 10 times; turn = 31 sts

Row 3: (RS) Ch 2, skip first st, [fpdc around next st, bpdc around next st] 14 times, fpdc around next st, dc in last st; turn = 31 sts

Row 4: (WS) Ch 2, skip first st, [bpdc around next st, fpdc around next st] 14 times, bpdc around next st, dc in last st, changing to **CC1**; turn without breaking off **MC** = 31 sts

Row 5: (RS) With **CC1**, ch 1 (does not count as a st now and throughout), sc in first st, PC in next st, [sc in next 3 sts, PC in next st] 7 times, sc in last st; turn = 8 PC and 23 sc

Row 6: (WS) Ch 1, sc in first st, sc in each st across, changing to **MC** at the end of the row; break off **CC1** and turn = 31 sts

Row 7: (RS) With **MC**, ch 2, skip first st, dc in next 30 sts, turn = 31 sts

Row 8: (WS) Same as Row 4

Row 9: (RS) Same as Row 3

Row 10: (WS) Ch 1, sc in first st, sc2tog, [sc in next st, sc2tog] 9 times, sc in last st = 21 sts

Fasten off, leaving a long tail for sewing.

HORN
Kids – S, M, L

HORN
Adults – S, M, L

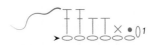

FINISHING FRILL

Fold the frill in half along the PC row and whipstitch across the left and right edges using the long **MC** tail on each side **(fig 1)**. Do not fasten off, but bring the tails through the stitches to the bottom edge to be used for future assembling.

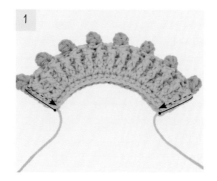

NOTE:
Diagrams show the RS of the work, therefore:

⊤ = *Fpdc on RS or bpdc on WS*

⊤ = *Bpdc on RS or fpdc on WS*

Finishing Slippers

Position the muzzle on the front of the slipper and backstitch around onto the slipper using the long **CC2** tail from the muzzle **(fig 2)**. Fasten off and weave in the end.

Position the first horn above the center of the muzzle, placing it right up against the edge. Using the long **CC3** tail from the horn, whipstitch across the bottom edge and backstitch around the remaining edges **(fig 2)**. Fasten off and weave in the end.

To finish the eyes, use 15mm buttons for Kids' sizes or 20mm buttons for Adults' sizes. Sew the buttons on each side of the gusset seams **(fig 2)**, placing them right up against the muzzle (*see Useful Information: Sewing Buttons*).

Position the frill along the top edge of the gusset and whipstitch across the front and back edges using the long **MC** tails from the frill **(fig 3)**. Fasten off and weave in the ends.

Using the gusset seams as guides, position the 2 remaining horns onto the front of the frill, placing them on each side of the gusset **(fig 4)**. Using the long tail from each horn, whipstitch across the bottom edge and backstitch around the remaining edges. Fasten off and weave in the ends.

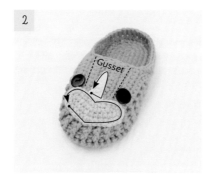

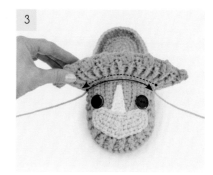

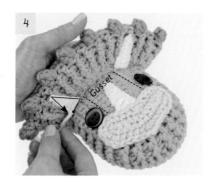

FRILL
Kids – S, M, L

Back - Bottom Edge

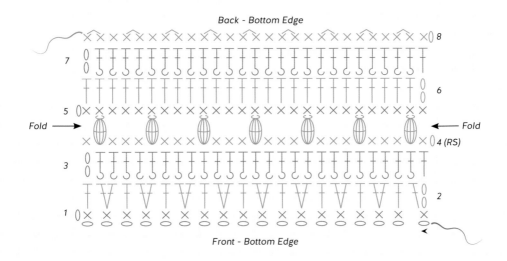

Front - Bottom Edge

FRILL
Adults – S, M, L

Back - Bottom Edge

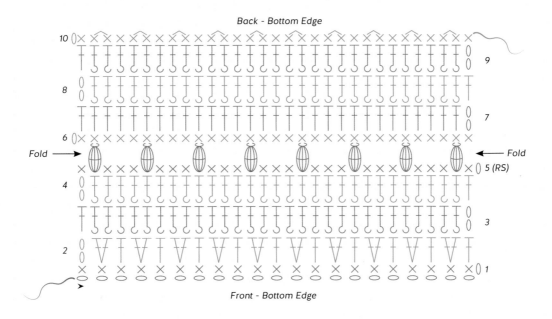

Front - Bottom Edge

the
Starry
Unicorn

* * * * * * * * * * * * * * * * *

Brighten up your day with a bit of unicorn magic!
They say unicorns are uncatchable, but you can make
your own unicorn slippers that will keep your toes
warm and your eyes sparkling.

Materials

YARN - WEIGHT 4

A small amount of **MC** (White) for ears,
CC1 (Bright Yellow or Metallic) for horn
and star, **CC2** (Variegated) for mane,
CC3 (Light Pink) for cheeks, **CC4**
(Black) for eyes.

Use **MC** (White) for the upper of
your slippers, **CC2** (Variegated) for
insoles and any matching solid color
for outsoles.

HOOKS

3.75mm (F), 4.25mm (G)

ADDITIONAL MATERIALS

- Stitch marker
- Polyester stuffing
- Fabric glue
- Tapestry needle and scissors

STITCH SUMMARY

Ch, sl st, sc, hdc, dc, sc2tog
(or invisible decrease), magic ring
(optional), join

SKILLS

Working in rows and in the round,
increasing, decreasing, sewing

Skill Level

●●●○

Ears

Make 2 for each slipper. Work in spiral rounds from the top down, using **MC** and a 4.25mm (G) hook. Use a stitch marker to mark the start of each round as you go.

KIDS – S, M, L

To beg: Ch 3, sl st in third ch from hook to form a ring (or start with a magic ring)

Rnd 1: Ch 1 (does not count as a st), 5 sc in ring; do not join now and throughout = 5 sts

Rnd 2: 2 sc in first st of previous rnd, 2 sc in next 4 sts = 10 sts

Rnds 3 – 4: Sc in each st around = 10 sts

Rnd 5: [Sc in next 4 sts, 2 sc in next st] 2 times = 12 sts

Rnds 6 – 7: Sc in each st around = 12 sts

Rnd 8: [Sc in next st, sc2tog] 4 times = 8 sts

Sl st in next st and fasten off, leaving a long tail for sewing.

ADULTS – S, M, L

To beg: Ch 3, sl st in third ch from hook to form a ring (or start with a magic ring)

Rnds 1 – 4: Same as for Kids

Rnd 5: [Sc in next st, 2 sc in next st] 5 times = 15 sts

Rnds 6 – 8: Sc in each st around = 15 sts

Rnd 9: [Sc in next st, sc2tog] 5 times = 10 sts

Sl st in next st and fasten off, leaving a long tail for sewing.

Mane

Make 2 sets of spirals for each slipper. Work in rows with **CC2** and a 4.25mm (G) hook.

KIDS – S, M, L

Row 1: (RS) Ch 13, 2 sc in second ch from hook (the skipped ch does not count as a st), 2 sc in each of next 11 chs; *do not break off yarn and do not turn** = 24 sts

Row 2: Same as Row 1, omitting instructions from * to **

Fasten off, leaving a long tail for sewing.

ADULTS – S, M, L

Row 1: (RS) Ch 16, 2 sc in second ch from hook (the skipped ch does not count as a st), 2 sc in each of next 14 chs; *do not break off yarn and do not turn** = 30 sts

Row 2: Same as Row 1, omitting instructions from * to **

Fasten off, leaving a long tail for sewing.

MANE
Kids – S, M, L

MANE
Adults – S, M, L

Cheeks

Make 2 for each slipper. Work in the round with **CC3** and a 4.25mm (G) hook.

KIDS – S, M, L

To beg: Ch 3, sl st in third ch from hook to form a ring (or start with a magic ring)

Rnd 1: Ch 1 (does not count as a st), 8 hdc in ring; join = 8 sts

Fasten off, leaving a long tail for sewing.

ADULTS – S, M, L

To beg: Ch 3, sl st in third ch from hook to form a ring (or start with a magic ring)

Rnd 1: Ch 2 (does not count as a st), 12 dc in ring; join = 12 sts

Fasten off, leaving a long tail for sewing.

Horn

Make 1 for each slipper. Work in spiral rounds from the bottom up, using **CC1** and a 3.75mm (F) hook. Use a stitch marker to mark the start of each round as you go.

KIDS – S, M, L

To beg: Ch 12, sl st in last ch from hook to form a ring, being careful not to twist the chain

Rnd 1: Ch 1 (does not count as a st), sc in same ch as join, sc in next 11 chs; do not join now and throughout = 12 sts

Rnd 2: Sc in first st of previous rnd, sc in next 11 sts = 12 sts

Rnds 3 – 4: Sc in each st around = 12 sts

Rnd 5: [Sc in next 2 sts, sc2tog] 3 times = 9 sts

Rnds 6 – 8: Sc in each st around = 9 sts

Rnd 9: [Sc in next st, sc2tog] 3 times = 6 sts

Rnds 10 – 12: Sc in each st around = 6 sts

Rnd 13: [Sc2tog] 2 times, skip st, sl st in last st, ch 45 = 3 sts and ch-45 tail

Fasten off, leaving a long tail for sewing.

ADULTS – S, M, L

To beg: Ch 15, sl st in last ch from hook to form a ring, being careful not to twist the chain

Rnd 1: Ch 1 (does not count as a st), sc in same ch as join, sc in next 14 chs; do not join now and throughout = 15 sts

Rnd 2: Sc in first st of previous rnd, sc in next 14 sts = 15 sts

Rnds 3 – 4: Sc in each st around = 15 sts

Rnd 5: [Sc in next 3 sts, sc2tog] 3 times = 12 sts

Rnds 6 – 8: Sc in each st around = 12 sts

Rnd 9: [Sc in next 2 sts, sc2tog] 3 times = 9 sts

Rnds 10 – 12: Sc in each st around = 9 sts

Rnd 13: [Sc in next st, sc2tog] 3 times = 6 sts

Rnds 14 – 16: Sc in each st around = 6 sts

Rnd 17: [Sc2tog] 2 times, skip st, sl st in last st, ch 60 = 3 sts and ch-60 tail

Fasten off, leaving a long tail for sewing.

CHEEK
Kids – S, M, L

CHEEK
Adults – S, M, L

STAR
All Sizes

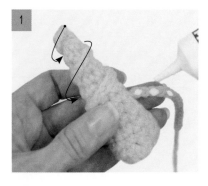

Tip

To make sparkling stars, use 2 or 3 strands of metallic thread held together.

FINISHING HORN

Stuff the horn firmly, using a chopstick or the tips of scissors for pushing polyester stuffing into the horn.

Wrap the long chain tail in spiral motion around the horn from the top down, applying fabric glue along the back side of the chain as you go **(fig 1)**. Once you reach the bottom edge, attach the end of the chain to the horn with a stitch marker and allow the glue to dry **(fig 2)**.

NOTE:

Be sure to check instructions on the glue label and test your fabric glue prior to using.

Star

Make 1 for each slipper. Work in the round with **CC1**, using a 3.75mm (F) hook for Kids' sizes or 4.25mm (G) hook for Adults' sizes.

To beg: Ch 3, sl st in third ch from hook to form a ring (or start with a magic ring)

Rnd 1: Ch 1 (does not count as a st), [sc in ring, ch 3, sl st in second ch from hook, sc in next ch] 5 times; join = 5 star points

Fasten off, leaving a long tail for sewing.

Finishing Slippers

Position the cheeks on each side of the slipper, approximately 1 row away from the gusset curve **(fig 3)**. Backstitch around onto the slipper using the long **CC3** tail from each cheek. Fasten off and weave in the ends.

Thread the tapestry needle with **CC4** and stitch smiley eyes above the cheeks (*see Useful Information: Sewing Techniques*), placing the inner edge of each eye by the gusset seam **(fig 4)**. Fasten off and weave in the ends.

Position the horn in the center of the gusset by the edge and whipstitch around onto the slipper using the long **CC1** tail from the horn **(fig 5)**. Fasten off and weave in the end.

Position the ears right up against the horn on each side and whipstitch around the bottom edge onto the slipper using the long **MC** tail from each ear **(figs 6 and 7)**. Fasten off and weave in the ends.

To finish the mane, position the first piece with 2 spirals in front of the ear. Using the long **CC2** tail, whipstitch across the raw edge to the horn **(fig 8)**. Fasten off and weave in the end.

Position the second piece with 2 spirals behind the same ear. Using the long **CC2** tail, whipstitch across the raw edge to the slipper **(fig 9)**. Fasten off and weave in the end.

Position the star by the ear without a mane, in front or behind the ear. Using the long **CC1** tail from the star, backstitch around the edge and whipstitch in each corner to keep the points of the star nice and sharp **(fig 10)**. Fasten off and weave in the end.

Finish your second slipper in the same manner but mirroring the placement of the mane and star.

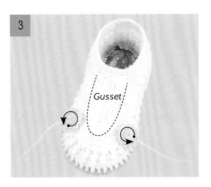

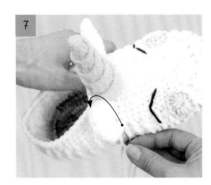

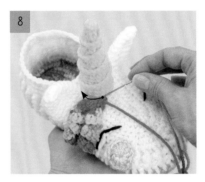

the Rock'n'Roll Panda

- - - - - - - -

Some pandas are quiet and shy while others are rock stars.
You can enjoy these cozy slippers in a traditional panda look or
add a bit of glamour by using a star-patch for the eyes.

Materials

YARN - WEIGHT 4

A small amount of **CC1** (Black) for ears,
patches and nose.

Use **MC** (White) for the upper of your
slippers, and use **CC1** (Black) for insoles
and outsoles.

HOOK

4.25mm (G)

ADDITIONAL MATERIALS

- Stitch marker
- Buttons for eyes: 4 x 10mm for Kids S
  (M, L) or 4 x 15mm for Adults S (M, L)
- White felt for highlighting eyes
- Sewing needle and thread
- Tapestry needle and scissors

STITCH SUMMARY

Ch, sl st, sc, hdc, dc, sc2tog (or
invisible decrease), magic ring
(optional), join

SKILLS

Working in rows and in the round,
working across the opposite side
of the foundation chain, increasing,
decreasing, sewing

Skill Level

Ears

Make 2 for each slipper. Work in spiral rounds from the top down using **CC1** and a 4.25mm (G) hook. Use a stitch marker to mark the start of each round as you go.

KIDS – S, M, L

To beg: Ch 3, sl st in third ch from hook to form a ring (or start with a magic ring)

Rnd 1: Ch 1 (does not count as a st), 6 sc in ring; do not join now and throughout = 6 sts

Rnd 2: 2 sc in first st of previous rnd, 2 sc in next 5 sts = 12 sts

Rnds 3 – 4: Sc in each st around = 12 sts

Rnd 5: [Sc in next st, sc2tog] 4 times = 8 sts

Sl st in next st and fasten off, leaving a long tail for sewing.

ADULTS – S, M, L

To beg: Ch 3, sl st in third ch from hook to form a ring (or start with a magic ring)

Rnds 1 – 2: Same as for Kids

Rnd 3: [Sc in next 3 sts, 2 sc in next st] 3 times = 15 sts

Rnds 4 – 5: Sc in each st around = 15 sts

Rnd 6: [Sc in next st, sc2tog] 5 times = 10 sts

Sl st in next st and fasten off, leaving a long tail for sewing.

Oval Patches

Make 1 for each rock 'n' roll panda or 2 for each traditional panda. Work in the round with **CC1** and a 4.25mm (G) hook.

KIDS – S, M, L

To beg: Ch 5

Rnd 1: Sc in second ch from hook (the skipped ch does not count as a st), sc in next ch, hdc in next ch, 4 hdc in last ch; working across the opposite side of the foundation ch, hdc in next ch, sc in next ch, 2 sc in last ch; join = 11 sts

Fasten off, leaving a long tail for sewing.

ADULTS – S, M, L

To beg: Ch 6

Rnd 1: Sc in second ch from hook (the skipped ch does not count as a st), hdc in next 2 chs, dc in next ch, 6 dc in last ch; working across the opposite side of the foundation ch, dc in next ch, hdc in next 2 chs, 2 sc in last ch; join = 15 sts

Fasten off, leaving a long tail for sewing.

Star Patches

Make 1 for each rock 'n' roll panda or omit stars for traditional pandas. Work in the round with **CC1** and a 4.25mm (G) hook.

KIDS – S, M, L

To beg: Ch 3, sl st in third ch from hook to form a ring (or start with a magic ring)

Rnd 1: Ch 1 (does not count as a st), [sc in ring, ch 3, sl st in second ch from hook, sc in next ch] 5 times; join = 5 star points

Fasten off, leaving a long tail for sewing.

ADULTS – S, M, L

To beg: Ch 3, sl st in third ch from hook to form a ring (or start with a magic ring)

Rnd 1: Ch 1 (does not count as a st), 6 sc in ring; join = 6 sts

Rnd 2: Skip st with join, [ch 4, sl st in second ch from hook, sc in next ch, hdc in next ch, sl st in next st of working rnd] 5 times = 5 star points

Fasten off, leaving a long tail for sewing.

OVAL PATCH
Kids - S, M, L

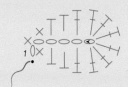

OVAL PATCH
Adults - S, M, L

STAR PATCH
Kids - S, M, L

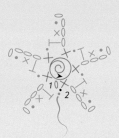

STAR PATCH
Adults - S, M, L

Finishing Slippers

To finish the eyes, use 10mm buttons for Kids' sizes or 15mm buttons for Adults' sizes, and add a white felt circle as a highlighting layer under each button. Sew the eyes to the narrow side of the oval patches or to the center of the star patch (see *Useful Information: Sewing Buttons*).

Using the gusset seams as guides, position the eye patches on each side of the gusset curve **(fig 1)**. You can finish traditional pandas using oval patches, or use oval and star patches to finish rock 'n' roll pandas. You can even make 1 slipper of each kind and create a unique pair.

Using the long **CC1** tail, backstitch around each patch onto the slipper **(figs 2 and 3)**. When you sew around the star edge, stop in each corner and whipstitch to keep the points nice and sharp. Fasten off and weave in the end.

Thread the tapestry needle with **CC1** and stitch a T-shaped nose between the patches **(fig 4)**, just above the gusset curve (see *Useful Information: Sewing Techniques*). Fasten off and weave in the end.

Holding the ears flat and with the opening facing down, position them on each side of the slipper, 1 row away from the gusset seams **(fig 5)**.

Using the long **CC1** tail, whipstitch around the bottom edge of each ear onto the slipper **(fig 6)**. Fasten off and weave in the ends.

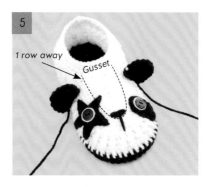

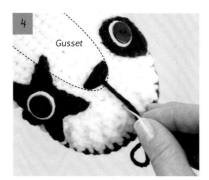

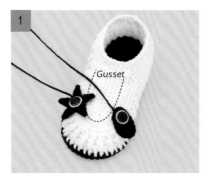

the Sleepy Koala

. . . .

As you know, long sleeps are essential for koalas.
These cute koala slippers will keep you snug as a bug
in a rug when you enjoy a sweet afternoon nap.

Materials

YARN - WEIGHT 4

A small amount of **MC** (Light Gray) for
outer ears, **CC1** (Black) for nose, **CC2**
(White or Light Pink) for inner ears.

Use **MC** (Light Gray) for the upper of
your slippers and outsoles, and use
CC2 (White or Light Pink) for insoles.

HOOK

4.25mm (G)

ADDITIONAL MATERIALS

- Buttons for eyes: 4 x 10mm for
  Kids S (M, L) or 4 x 15mm for Adults
  S (M, L)
- Sewing needle and thread
- Tapestry needle and scissors

STITCH SUMMARY

Ch, sl st, sc, hdc, magic ring
(optional), join

SKILLS

Working in rows and in the round,
working across the opposite
side of the foundation chain,
increasing, sewing

Skill Level

Ears

Make 2 for each slipper. Work in rows with a 4.25mm (G) hook.

KIDS – S, M, L

INNER EAR:

For each ear, make 1 inner ear using **CC2**.

To beg: Ch 3, sl st in third ch from hook to form a ring (or start with a magic ring)

Row 1: Ch 1 (does not count as a st now and throughout), 4 sc in ring; turn = 4 sts

Row 2: Ch 1, 2 sc in first st, 2 sc in each of next 3 sts; turn = 8 sts

Row 3: Ch 1, 2 sc in first st, sc in next st, [2 sc in next st, sc in next st] 3 times = 12 sts

Fasten off and weave in the ends.

OUTER EAR:

For each ear, make 1 outer ear using **MC**. Work same as inner ear but do not fasten off. Turn and proceed to joining row.

JOINING ROW:

Place the inner ear on top of the outer ear with WS facing each other and work the next row through both pieces at the same time, using the working yarn from the outer ear.

Row 4: (RS) Ch 1, sc in each st across = 12 sts

Fasten off, leaving a long tail for sewing.

ADULTS – S, M, L

INNER EAR:

For each ear, make 1 inner ear using **CC2**.

To beg: Ch 3, sl st in third ch from hook to form a ring (or start with a magic ring)

Rows 1 – 3: Same as for Kids; turn

Row 4: Ch 1, 2 sc in first st, sc in next 2 sts, [2 sc in next st, sc in next 2 sts] 3 times = 16 sts

Fasten off and weave in the ends.

OUTER EAR:

For each ear, make 1 outer ear using **MC**. Work same as inner ear but do not fasten off. Turn and proceed to joining row.

JOINING ROW:

Place the inner ear on top of the outer ear with WS facing each other and work the next row through both pieces at the same time, using the working yarn from the outer ear.

Row 5: (RS) Ch 1, sc in each st across = 16 sts

Fasten off, leaving a long tail for sewing.

Nose

Make 1 for each slipper. Work in the round with **CC1** and a 4.25mm (G) hook.

KIDS – S, M, L

To beg: Ch 5

Rnd 1: Hdc in second ch from hook (the skipped ch does not count as a st), hdc in next 2 chs, 4 hdc in last ch; working across the opposite side of the foundation ch, hdc in next 2 chs, 3 hdc in last ch; join = 12 sts

Fasten off, leaving a long tail for sewing.

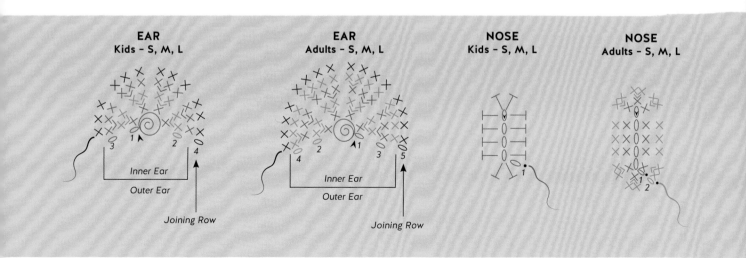

EAR
Kids – S, M, L

Inner Ear
Outer Ear
Joining Row

EAR
Adults – S, M, L

Inner Ear
Outer Ear
Joining Row

NOSE
Kids – S, M, L

NOSE
Adults – S, M, L

ADULTS - S, M, L

To beg: Ch 6

Rnd 1: Sc in second ch from hook (the skipped ch does not count as a st), sc in next 3 chs, 3 sc in last ch; working across the opposite side of the foundation ch, sc in next 3 chs, 2 sc in last ch; join = 12 sts

Rnd 2: Ch 1 (does not count as a st), 2 sc in same st as join, sc in next 3 sts, 2 sc in each of next 3 sts, sc in next 3 sts, 2 sc in each of next 2 sts; join = 18 sts

Fasten off, leaving a long tail for sewing.

Finishing Slippers

Position the nose on the front of the slipper and backstitch around onto the slipper using the long **CC1** tail **(fig 1)**. Fasten off and weave in the end.

To finish the eyes, use 10mm buttons for Kids' sizes or 15mm buttons for Adults' sizes. Sew the buttons on each side of the gusset seams **(fig 2)**, leveling them up with the top of the nose (*see Useful Information: Sewing Buttons*).

Position the ears slightly slanted along each side of the slipper, placing the top corners of the ears 2 rows away from the gusset seams **(fig 2)**. Whipstitch the ears around the bottom edge, using the long **MC** tail from each ear **(fig 3)**. Fasten off and weave in the ends.

To finish hair, prepare 3 bundles of **MC** yarn with 5 strands in each bundle: Wrap yarn 5 times around 4 fingers and cut the wraps on 1 side (1 bundle made).

Insert the hook through the stitches of the center row of the gusset, fold the yarn bundle in half and pull it through, creating a loop **(fig 4)**. Pull the yarn ends through the loop and tighten them (first tassel made). Attach the second and third tassels in the same manner, placing them on each side of the first tassel. Trim the ends to desired length **(fig 5)**.

2 rows away

Gusset

the Mossy Sloth

No rush, no worries, be mellow, chilled and relaxed, just like the mossy sloth. When you enjoy a cup of eucalyptus tea, these cozy sloth slippers will help you to stay warm and calm.

Materials

YARN - WEIGHT 4

A small amount of **CC1** (Beige) for face, **CC2** (Coffee) for eyes, **CC3** (Green) for ties.

Use **MC** (Taupe) or any other neutral earthy color for the upper of your slippers and outsoles, and use **CC1** (Beige) for insoles.

HOOK

4.25mm (G)

ADDITIONAL MATERIALS

- 4 wooden craft beads for ties, approximately 10mm diameter
- Tapestry needle and scissors

STITCH SUMMARY

Ch, sl st, sc, join

SKILLS

Working in rows and in the round, working across the opposite side of the foundation chain, increasing, sewing

Skill Level

Face

Make 1 for each slipper. Work in the round with **CC1** and a 4.25mm (G) hook.

KIDS – S, M, L

To beg: Ch 8

Rnd 1: Sc in second ch from hook (the skipped ch does not count as a st), sc in next 5 chs, 3 sc in last ch; working across the opposite side of the foundation ch, sc in next 5 chs, 2 sc in last ch; join = 16 sts

Rnd 2: Ch 1 (does not count as a st now and throughout), 2 sc in same st as join, sc in next 5 sts, 2 sc in each of next 3 sts, sc in next 5 sts, 2 sc in each of next 2 sts; join = 22 sts

Rnd 3: Ch 1, sc in same st as join, 2 sc in next st, sc in next 5 sts, [sc in next st, 2 sc in next st] 3 times, sc in next 5 sts, [sc in next st, 2 sc in next st] 2 times; join = 28 sts

Fasten off, leaving a long tail for sewing.

ADULTS – S, M, L

To beg: Ch 8

Rnds 1 – 3: Same as for Kids

Rnd 4: Ch 1, 2 sc in same st as join, sc in next 7 sts, [2 sc in next st, sc in each of next 2 sts] 3 times, sc in next 5 sts, [2 sc in next st, sc in each of next 2 sts] 2 times; join = 34 sts

Fasten off, leaving a long tail for sewing.

Eye Patches

Make 2 for each slipper. Work in the round with **CC2** and a 4.25mm (G) hook.

KIDS – S, M, L

To beg: Ch 6

Rnd 1: Sc in second ch from hook (the skipped ch does not count as a st), sc in next 3 chs, 3 sc in last ch; working across the opposite side of the foundation ch, sc in next 3 chs, 2 sc in last ch; join = 12 sts

Fasten off, leaving a long tail for sewing.

ADULTS – S, M, L

To beg: Ch 5

Rnd 1: Sc in second ch from hook (the skipped ch does not count as a st), sc in next 2 chs, 3 sc in last ch; working across the opposite side of the foundation ch, sc in next 2 chs, 2 sc in last ch; join = 10 sts

Rnd 2: Ch 1 (does not count as a st), 2 sc in same st as join, sc in next 2 sts, 2 sc in each of next 3 sts, sc in next 2 sts, 2 sc in each of next 2 sts; join = 16 sts

Fasten off, leaving a long tail for sewing.

Ties

Optional - make 2 for each slipper. Work with **CC3** and a 4.25mm (G) hook.

- For Kids S (M, L) – Ch 30
- For Adults S (M, L) – Ch 35

Fasten off, leaving a long tail for sewing. Add a wooden bead at the beginning of the chain and tie a firm knot to secure the bead. Trim off the end from the beginning.

NOTE:
If making for young children, do not use beads.

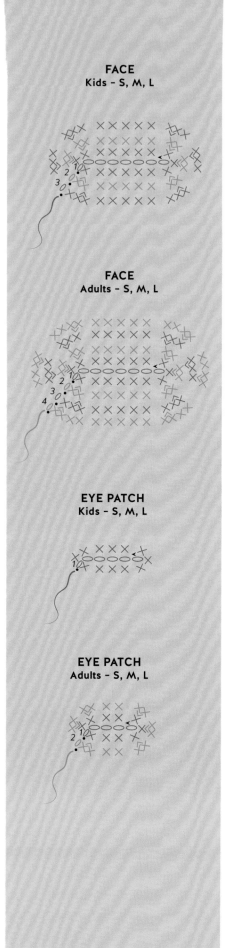

FACE
Kids – S, M, L

FACE
Adults – S, M, L

EYE PATCH
Kids – S, M, L

EYE PATCH
Adults – S, M, L

Finishing Slippers

Thread the tapestry needle with **CC2** and whipstitch 3-4 times across 3 stitches in the center of the face to create the nose. Using the same yarn, backstitch a crooked smile below the nose **(fig 1)**. Fasten off and weave in the end.

Position the face on the front of the slipper and backstitch around onto the slipper using the long **CC1** tail from the face **(fig 1)**. Fasten off and weave in the end.

Thread the tapestry needle with **CC1** and stitch sleepy eyes across the center of each eye patch (*see Useful Information: Sewing Techniques*). Fasten off and weave in the ends.

Position the patches on each side of the face, slanting them from the center round of the face down to the sides **(fig 2)**. Backstitch around, using the long **CC2** tail from the patches **(fig 3)**. Fasten off and weave in the ends.

To finish ties, use the long **CC3** tail to sew them on each side of the slipper by whipstitching across 2-3 chains **(fig 4)**. Fasten off and weave in the ends. Tie a bow when wearing.

NOTE:
If making for young children, tie the bow and stitch in place.

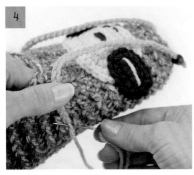

Tip

For a different look, position the face upside down and your mossy sloths will always look towards you.

the Graceful Elephant

- - - - - - - -

Baby elephants are the cutest animals of all! They are playful, graceful and incredibly cute. Make a pair of elephant slippers to warm up your feet and your heart.

Materials

YARN - WEIGHT 4

A small amount of **MC** (Light Gray) for ears, trunk and hair.

Use **MC** (Light Gray) for the upper of your slippers and outsoles, and use **CC** (White) for insoles.

HOOKS

3.75mm (F), 4.25mm (G), 5mm (H)

ADDITIONAL MATERIALS

- Stitch marker
- Buttons for eyes: 4 x 15mm for Kids S (M, L) or 4 x 20mm for Adults S (M, L)
- Sewing needle and thread
- Tapestry needle and scissors

STITCH SUMMARY

Ch, sl st, sc, hdc, dc, picot, shell, arch, join

SKILLS

Working in rows and in the round, increasing, sewing

Skill Level

●●○○

Ears

Make 2 for each slipper. Work in rows with **MC** using a 3.75mm (F) hook for Kids' sizes or 5mm (H) hook for Adults' sizes.

To beg: Ch 2

Row 1: (RS) 3 sc in second ch from hook (the skipped ch does not count as a st); turn = 3 sts

Row 2: (WS) Ch 1 (does not count as a st now and throughout), 2 sc in first st, 2 sc in each of next 2 sts; turn = 6 sts

Row 3: (RS) Ch 1, 2 sc in first st, sc in next st, [2 sc in next st, sc in next st] 2 times; turn = 9 sts

Row 4: (WS) Ch 2 (counts as dc), dc in first st, [ch 3, skip st, 2 dc in next st, dc in next st] 2 times, ch 3, skip st, 2 dc in last st; turn = 10 sts and 3 arches

Row 5: (RS) Skip 2 dc, *shell in next arch, [skip st, sl st in next st, skip st, shell in next arch] 2 times, skip st, sl st in last st = 3 shells

NOTE:
*Shell = [2 dc, picot] 3 times, dc

Fasten off, leaving a long tail for sewing.

Trunk

Make 1 for each slipper. Work in spiral rounds from the bottom up, using **MC** and a 4.25mm (G) hook. Use a stitch marker to indicate the start of each round as you go.

KIDS – S, M, L

To beg: Ch 10, sl st in last ch from hook to form a ring, being careful not to twist the chain

Rnd 1: Ch 1 (does not count as a st), sc in each ch around the ring; do not join now and throughout = 10 sts

Rnd 2: Sc in first st of previous rnd, sc in next 9 sts = 10 sts

Rnds 3 – 9: Sc in next 3 sts, hdc in next 4 sts, sc in next 3 sts = 10 sts

Rnd 10: 2 sc in each st around = 20 sts

Rnd 11: Sc in each st around = 20 sts

Sl st in next st and fasten off, leaving a long tail for sewing.

ADULTS – S, M, L

To beg: Ch 12, sl st in last ch from hook to form a ring, being careful not to twist the chain.

Rnd 1: Ch 1 (does not count as a st), sc in each ch around the ring; do not join now and throughout = 12 sts

Rnd 2: Sc in first st of previous rnd, sc in next 11 sts = 12 sts

Rnds 3 – 10: Sc in next 3 sts, hdc in next 6 sts, sc in next 3 sts = 12 sts

Rnd 11: 2 sc in each st around = 24 sts

Rnd 12: Sc in each st around = 24 sts

Sl st in next st and fasten off, leaving a long tail for sewing.

EAR
All Sizes

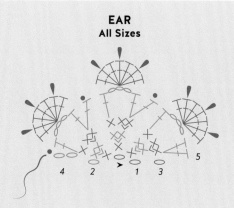

Finishing Slippers

With the trunk curved to the side, hold the top edge of the trunk folded flat. Using the long **MC** tail, whipstitch across the top edge to close the opening **(fig 1)**. Do not fasten off just yet.

Position the trunk on the front of the slipper and whipstitch across the top edge using **MC (fig 2)**. Fasten off and weave in the end.

To finish the eyes, use 15mm buttons for Kids' sizes or 20mm buttons for Adults' sizes. Sew the buttons on each side of the gusset seams **(fig 3)**, placing them right up against the trunk (*see Useful Information: Sewing Buttons*).

With RS facing, position the ears along each side of the slipper, leveling up the center of the ears with the eyes **(fig 3)**. Whipstitch the ears across the bottom edge on WS, using the long **MC** tail from each ear **(fig 4)**. Do not sew on RS. Fasten off and weave in the ends.

To finish hair, prepare 3 bundles of **MC** yarn with 5 strands in each bundle: Wrap yarn 5 times around 4 fingers and cut the wraps on 1 side (1 bundle made).

Insert the hook through the stitches of the center row of the gusset, fold the yarn bundle in half and pull it through, creating a loop **(fig 5)**. Pull the yarn ends through the loop and tighten them (first tassel made). Attach the second and third tassels in the same manner, placing them on each side of the first tassel. Trim the ends to desired length **(fig 6)**.

Finish your second slipper in the same manner but mirror the curve of the trunk **(fig 2)**.

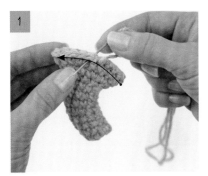

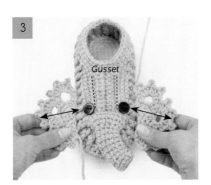

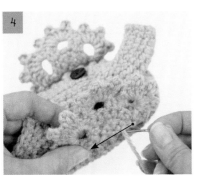

Gusset

the Playful Pig

❋ ❋ ❋ ❋ ❋ ❋ ❋ ❋ ❋ ❋ ❋ ❋ ❋ ❋ ❋ ❋ ❋ ❋ ❋

Playful squealing piggies are too cute for words.
Don't worry if they get a little muddy from zig-zagging
around. These slippers are easy to wash and care for,
following the care instructions (see Useful Information).

Materials

YARN - WEIGHT 4

A small amount of **MC** (Pretty Pink) for
ears and tail, **CC1** (Dusty Pink)
for snout.

Use **MC** (Pretty Pink) for the upper of
your slippers and outsoles, and use any
contrasting color for insoles

HOOK

4.25mm (G)

ADDITIONAL MATERIALS

• Stitch marker
• Buttons for eyes: 4 x 10mm for
  Kids S (M, L) or 4 x 15mm for Adults
  S (M, L)
• Sewing needle and thread
• Tapestry needle and scissors

STITCH SUMMARY

Ch, sl st, sc, sc2tog (or invisible
decrease), rsc, hdc, dc, magic ring
(optional), join

SKILLS

Working in rows and in the round,
working across the opposite side
of the foundation chain, increasing,
decreasing, sewing

Skill Level

Snout

Make 1 for each slipper. Work in the round with **CC1** and a 4.25mm (G) hook.

KIDS – S, M, L

To beg: Ch 6

Rnd 1: Sc in second ch from hook (the skipped ch does not count as a st), sc in next 3 chs, 3 sc in last ch; working across the opposite side of the foundation ch, sc in next 3 chs, 2 sc in last ch; join = 12 sts

Rnd 2: Ch 1 (does not count as a st now and throughout), 2 sc in same st as join, sc in next 3 sts, 2 sc in each of next 3 sts, sc in next 3 sts, 2 sc in each of next 2 sts; join = 18 sts

Rnd 3: Ch 1, rsc in each st around; join = 18 sts

Fasten off, leaving a long tail for sewing.

ADULTS – S, M, L

To beg: Ch 6

Rnds 1 - 2: Same as for Kids

Rnd 3: Sc in same st as join, 2 sc in next st, sc in next 3 sts, [sc in next st, 2 sc in next st] 3 times, sc in next 3 sts, [sc in next st, 2 sc in next st] 2 times; join = 24 sts

Rnd 4: Ch 1, rsc in each st around; join = 24 sts

Fasten off, leaving a long tail for sewing.

Ears

Make 2 for each slipper. Work in spiral rounds from the top down using **MC** and a 4.25mm (G) hook. Use a stitch marker to mark the start of each round as you go.

KIDS - S, M, L

To beg: Ch 3, sl st in third ch from hook to form a ring (or start with a magic ring)

Rnd 1: Ch 1 (does not count as a st), 5 sc in ring; do not join now and throughout = 5 sts

Rnd 2: Sc in first st of previous rnd, sc in next 4 sts = 5 sts

Rnd 3: 2 sc in each st around = 10 sts

Rnd 4: Sc in each st around = 10 sts

Rnd 5: [Sc in next st, 2 sc in next st] 5 times = 15 sts

Rnds 6 - 9: Sc in each st around = 15 sts

Rnd 10: [Sc in next st, sc2tog] 5 times = 10 sts

Sl st in next st and fasten off, leaving a long tail for sewing.

ADULTS - S, M, L

To beg: Ch 3, sl st in third ch from hook to form a ring (or start with a magic ring)

Rnds 1 - 6: Same as for Kids

Rnd 7: [Sc in next 4 sts, 2 sc in next st] 3 times = 18 sts

Rnds 8 - 11: Sc in each st around = 18 sts

Rnd 12: [Sc in next st, sc2tog] 6 times = 12 sts

Sl st in next st and fasten off, leaving a long tail for sewing.

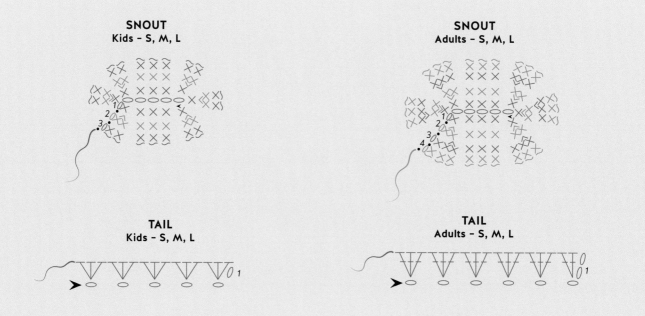

SNOUT
Kids – S, M, L

SNOUT
Adults – S, M, L

TAIL
Kids – S, M, L

TAIL
Adults – S, M, L

Tail

Make 1 for each slipper.
Work in rows with **MC** and a
4.25mm (G) hook.

KIDS – S, M, L

To beg: Ch 6

Row 1: (RS) 3 hdc in second ch
from hook (the skipped ch does
not count as a st), 3 hdc in each of
next 4 chs = 15 sts

Fasten off, leaving a long tail
for sewing.

ADULTS – S, M, L

To beg: Ch 8

Row 1: (RS) 2 dc in third ch from
hook (2 skipped chs count as dc),
3 dc in each of next 5 chs = 18 sts

Fasten off, leaving a long tail
for sewing.

Finishing Slippers

Thread the tapestry needle with
MC and stitch 2 nostrils on the
snout **(fig 1)**. Fasten off and weave
in the ends.

Position the snout on the front of
the slipper and backstitch around
onto the slipper using the long **CC1**
tail **(fig 2)**. Fasten off and weave in
the end.

To finish the eyes, use 10mm
buttons for Kids' sizes or 15mm
buttons for Adults' sizes. Sew
the buttons on each side of the
gusset seams, placing them right
up against the snout (*see Useful
Information: Sewing Buttons*).

Using the gusset seams as guides,
position the ears on each side of
the gusset **(fig 3)**.

Whipstitch the ears around the
bottom edge onto the slipper,
using the long **MC** tail from each
ear **(fig 4)**. Fasten off and weave in
the ends.

Position the tail on the back of
the slipper and whipstitch around
onto the slipper using the long **MC**
tail **(fig 5)**. Fasten off and weave in
the end.

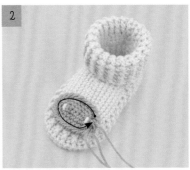

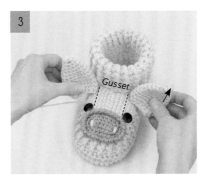

the Mischievous Raccoon

Sometimes it's fun to be mischievous like a raccoon and enjoy a late night snack. These soft crochet slippers will make your steps quiet when you want to sneak out to the kitchen unnoticed.

Materials

YARN - WEIGHT 4

A small amount of **MC** (Gray) for outer ears, **CC1** (Black) for inner ears and face, **CC2** (White) for face.

Use **MC** (Gray) for the upper of your slippers and outsoles, and use **CC1** (Black) for insoles.

HOOK

4.25mm (G)

ADDITIONAL MATERIALS

- Stitch markers
- Buttons for eyes: 4 x 10mm for Kids S (M, L) or 4 x 15mm for Adults S (M, L)
- White felt for highlighting eyes
- Sewing needle and thread
- Tapestry needle and scissors

STITCH SUMMARY

Ch, sl st, sc, hdc, dc, join

SKILLS

Working in rows, working across the opposite side of the foundation chain, raw edge finishing, increasing, sewing

Skill Level

Face

Make 1 for each slipper. Begin by working the muzzle in rows with **CC2** and a 4.25mm (G) hook.

KIDS – S, M, L

To beg: With **CC2**, ch 2

Row 1: 3 sc in second ch from hook (the skipped ch does not count as a st); turn = 3 sts

Row 2: Ch 1 (does not count as a st now and throughout), 2 sc in first st, 3 sc in next st, 2 sc in last st; turn = 7 sts

Row 3: Ch 1, 2 sc in first st, sc in next 2 sts, 3 sc in next st, sc in next 2 sts, 2 sc in last st; turn = 11 sts

Row 4: Ch 1, sc in first st and place **Marker A** in st just made, sc in next 4 sts, 3 sc in next st and place **Marker B** in last st made, sc in next 5 sts; do not turn = 13 sts

Edging: (RS) Rotate your work; ch 1, sc evenly across the bottom edge of the muzzle; join in **Marker A**, changing to **CC1 (fig 1)**

Break off **CC2**, leaving a long tail for sewing and continue to work the eye patches in rows **(figs 2 and 3)**:

Row 5: (RS) With **CC1**, ch 1, sc in same st with marker and remove the marker, sc in next 5 sts; turn = 6 sts

Row 6: (WS) Ch 3 (counts as dc), skip first st, dc in next 5 sts, changing to **CC2** at the end of the row; break off **CC1** and turn = 6 sts

Row 7: (RS) With **CC2**, ch 1, sc in first st, sc in next 5 sts; fasten off, leaving a long tail for sewing = 6 sts

With RS facing, join **CC1** in st with **Marker B** and repeat Rows 5–7. You should have 3 long **CC2** tails once finished. Weave in all the other ends.

ADULTS – S, M, L

To beg: With **CC2**, ch 2

Rows 1 - 3: Same as for Kids

Row 4: Ch 1, 2 sc in first st, sc in next 4 sts, 3 sc in next st, sc in next 4 sts, 2 sc in last st; turn = 15 sts

Row 5: Ch 1, sc in first st and place **Marker A** in st just made, sc in next 6 sts, 3 sc in next st and place **Marker B** in last st made, sc in next 7 sts; do not turn = 17 sts

Edging: (RS) Rotate your work; ch 1, sc evenly across the bottom edge of the muzzle; join in **Marker A**, changing to **CC1 (fig 1)**

Break off **CC2**, leaving a long tail for sewing and continue to work the eye patches in rows **(figs 2 and 3)**:

Row 6: (RS) With **CC1**, ch 1, sc in same st with marker and remove the marker, sc in next 7 sts; turn = 8 sts

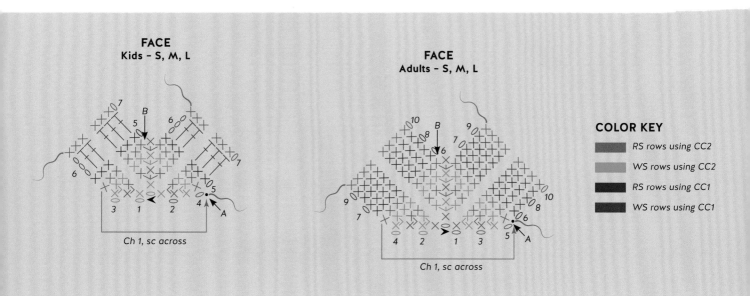

FACE
Kids – S, M, L

Ch 1, sc across

FACE
Adults – S, M, L

Ch 1, sc across

COLOR KEY

RS rows using CC2
WS rows using CC2
RS rows using CC1
WS rows using CC1

Rows 7 - 9: Ch 1, sc in first st, sc in next 7 sts; turn (change to **CC2** and break off **CC1** at the end of Row 9) = 8 sts

Row 10: (RS) With **CC2**, ch 1, sc in first st, sc in next 7 sts; fasten off, leaving a long tail for sewing = 8 sts

With RS facing, join **CC1** in st with **Marker B** and repeat Rows 6–10. You should have 3 long **CC2** tails once finished. Weave in all the other ends.

Ears

For each slipper, make 2 inner ears using **CC1** and 2 outer ears using **MC**. Work in rows with a 4.25mm (G) hook, following the same instructions for the inner and outer ears.

KIDS - S, M, L

To beg: Ch 4

Row 1: (WS) Sc in second ch from hook (the skipped ch does not count as a st), sc in next ch, 3 sc in last ch; working across the opposite side of the foundation ch, sc in next 2 chs; turn = 7 sts

Row 2: (RS) Ch 1 (does not count as a st), sc in first st, sc in next st, 2 sc in next st, (sc, hdc, sc) in next st, 2 sc in next st, sc in next 2 sts = 11 sts

Fasten off, leaving a long tail for sewing outer ears and weave in all the ends of inner ears.

ADULTS - S, M, L

To beg: Ch 5

Row 1: (RS) Sc in second ch from hook (the skipped ch does not count as a st), sc in next 2 chs, 3 sc in last ch; working across the opposite side of the foundation ch, sc in next 3 chs; turn = 9 sts

Row 2: (WS) Ch 1 (does not count as a st now and throughout), sc in first st, sc in next 2 sts, 2 sc in next st, (sc, hdc, sc) in next st, 2 sc in next st, sc in next 3 sts = 13 sts

Row 3: (RS) Ch 1, sc in first st, sc in next 4 sts, 2 sc in next st, (sc, hdc, sc) in next st, 2 sc in next st, sc in next 5 sts = 17 sts

Fasten off, leaving a long tail for sewing outer ears and weave in all the ends of inner ears.

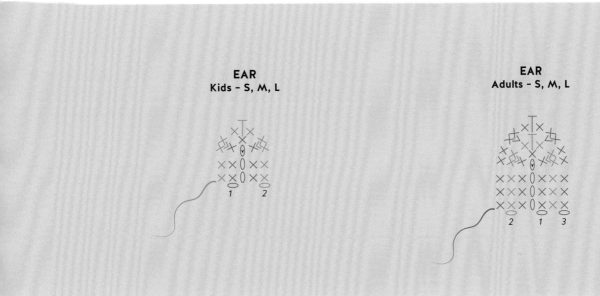

EAR
Kids - S, M, L

EAR
Adults - S, M, L

Finishing Slippers

Thread the tapestry needle with **CC1** and stitch a T-shaped nose on the muzzle (*See Useful Information: Sewing Techniques*). Fasten off and weave in the end. To finish the eyes, use 10mm buttons for Kids' sizes or 15mm buttons for Adults' sizes. Sew the buttons to the eye patches, adding a white felt circle as a highlight under each button (*see Useful Information: Sewing Buttons*).

Position the face on the front of the slipper and backstitch around the white muzzle using the long **CC2** tail **(fig 4)**. Fasten off and weave in the end. Using the remaining 2 tails, backstitch across the last row of each eye patch, leaving the side edges unstitched **(fig 4)**. Fasten off and weave in the ends.

Holding the inner and outer ears together, with WS facing each other, whipstitch across the last row using the long **MC** tail from the outer ears **(fig 5)**. Do not break off **MC**. Position the ears on each side of the gusset seams and whipstitch around onto the slipper using the long **MC** tail from each ear **(fig 6)**. Fasten off and weave in the ends.

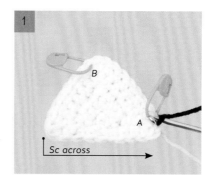

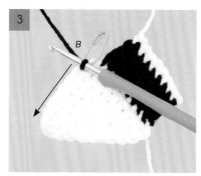

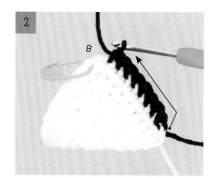

the Cheeky Monkey

Keep the troop warm and cozy for your next family gathering. They will go bananas over these fun, cheeky monkey slippers.

Materials

YARN - WEIGHT 4

A small amount of **MC** (Chocolate) for ears, hair and nostrils, **CC1** (Beige) for muzzle, **CC2** (Red) for smile.

Use **MC** (Chocolate) for the upper of your slippers and outsoles, and use **CC1** (Beige) for insoles.

HOOK

4.25mm (G)

ADDITIONAL MATERIALS

- Buttons for eyes: 4 x 10mm for Kids S (M, L) or 4 x 15mm for Adults S (M, L)
- White felt for highlighting eyes
- Sewing needle and thread
- Tapestry needle and scissors

STITCH SUMMARY

Ch, sl st, sc, rsc, magic ring (optional), join

SKILLS

Working in rows and in the round, working across the opposite side of the foundation chain, increasing, sewing

Skill Level

Muzzle

Make 1 for each slipper. Work in the round with **CC1** and a 4.25mm (G) hook.

KIDS – S, M, L

To beg: Ch 9

Rnd 1: Sc in second ch from hook (the skipped ch does not count as a st), sc in next 6 chs, 3 sc in last ch; working across the opposite side of the foundation ch, sc in next 6 chs, 2 sc in last ch; join = 18 sts

Rnd 2: Ch 1 (does not count as a st) 2 sc in same st as join, sc in next 6 sts, 2 sc in each of next 3 sts, sc in next 6 sts, 2 sc in each of next 2 sts; join = 24 sts

Fasten off, leaving a long tail for sewing.

ADULTS – S, M, L

To beg: Ch 10

Rnd 1: Sc in second ch from hook (the skipped ch does not count as a st), sc in next 7 chs, 3 sc in last ch; working across the opposite side of the foundation ch, sc in next 7 chs, 2 sc in last ch; join = 20 sts

Rnd 2: Ch 1 (does not count as a st now and throughout) 2 sc in same st as join, sc in next 7 sts, 2 sc in each of next 3 sts, sc in next 7 sts, 2 sc in each of next 2 sts; join = 26 sts

Rnd 3: Sc in same st as join, 2 sc in next st, sc in next 7 sts, [sc in next st, 2 sc in next st] 3 times, sc in next 7 sts, [sc in next st, 2 sc in next st] 2 times; join = 32 sts

Fasten off, leaving a long tail for sewing.

Ears

Make 2 for each slipper. Work in rows with **MC** and a 4.25mm (G) hook.

KIDS – S, M, L

To beg: Ch 3, sl st in third ch from hook to form a ring (or start with a magic ring)

Row 1: Ch 1 (does not count as a st now and throughout), 4 sc in ring; turn = 4 sts

Row 2: Ch 1, 2 sc in first st, 2 sc in each of next 3 sts; do not turn = 8 sts

Row 3: (RS) Ch 1, skip first st, rsc in next 6 sts, sl st in last st = 7 sts

Fasten off, leaving a long tail for sewing.

ADULTS – S, M, L

To beg: Ch 3, sl st in third ch from hook to form a ring (or start with a magic ring)

Rows 1 - 2: Same as for Kids; turn

Row 3: Ch 1, 2 sc in first st, sc in next st, [2 sc in next st, sc in next st] 3 times; do not turn = 12 sts

Row 4: (RS) Ch 1, skip first st, rsc in next 10 sts, sl st in last st = 11 sts

Fasten off, leaving a long tail for sewing.

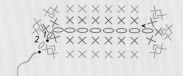

MUZZLE
Kids – S, M, L

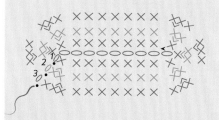

MUZZLE
Adults – S, M, L

EAR
Kids – S, M, L

EAR
Adults – S, M, L

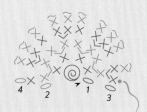

Finishing Slippers

To finish the muzzle, thread the tapestry needle with **MC** and cross stitch 2 nostrils, then thread the tapestry needle with **CC2** and backstitch a crooked smile. Fasten off and weave in the ends. Position the muzzle on the front of the slipper and backstitch around onto the slipper using the long **CC1** tail **(fig 1)**. Fasten off and weave in the end.

To finish the eyes, use 10mm buttons for Kids' sizes or 15mm buttons for Adults' sizes. Sew the buttons inside the gusset seams, placing them right up against the muzzle **(fig 2)** and adding a white felt circle as a highlighting layer under each button (*see Useful Information: Sewing Buttons*). Fasten off and weave in the ends.

With RS facing, position the ears along each side of the slipper, lining up the center of the ears with the eyes **(fig 3)**. Whipstitch the ears around the bottom edge, using the long **MC** tail from each ear **(fig 4)**. Fasten off and weave in the ends.

To finish hair, prepare 3 bundles of **MC** yarn with 5 strands in each bundle: Wrap yarn 5 times around 4 fingers and cut the wraps on 1 side (1 bundle made).

Insert the hook through the stitches of the center row of the gusset, fold the yarn bundle in half and pull it through, creating a loop **(fig 5)**. Pull the yarn ends through the loop and tighten them (first tassel made). Attach the second and third tassels in the same manner, placing them on each side of the first tassel. Trim the ends to the desired length **(fig 6)**.

the Woolly Sheep

Soft like a cloud, these woolly sheep slippers will keep your feet incredibly cozy when you are working on your next crochet project. It's never a baa-d idea to have an extra pair of slippers.

Materials

YARN - WEIGHT 4

A small amount of **MC** (Natural White) for hair, **CC1** (Light Gray) for face and ears, **CC2** (Black) for nose.

Use **MC** (Natural White) for the upper of your slippers, and use **CC1** (Light Gray) for insoles and outsoles.

HOOK

4.25mm (G)

ADDITIONAL MATERIALS

· Buttons for eyes: 4 x 10mm for Kids S (M, L) or 4 x 15mm for Adults S (M, L)
· Sewing needle and thread
· Tapestry needle and scissors

STITCH SUMMARY

Ch, sc, hdc, dc, lp

SKILLS

Working in rows, working across the opposite side of the foundation chain, increasing, sewing

Skill Level
●●●○

Face

Make 1 for each slipper.
Work in rows with **CC1** and a
4.25mm (G) hook.

KIDS – S, M, L

To beg: Ch 6

Row 1: (RS) Sc in second ch from hook (the skipped ch does not count as a st), sc in next 3 chs, 3 sc in last ch; working across the opposite side of the foundation ch, sc in next 4 chs; turn = 11 sts

Row 2: (WS) Ch 1 (does not count as a st now and throughout), sc in first st, sc in next 3 sts, 2 sc in each of next 3 sts, sc in next 4 sts; turn = 14 sts

Row 3: (RS) Ch 1, sc in first st, sc in next 3 sts, [2 sc in next st, sc in next st] 3 times, sc in next 4 sts; turn = 17 sts

Row 4: (WS) Ch 1, sc in first st, sc in next 3 sts, [2 sc in next st, sc in next 2 sts] 3 times, sc in next 4 sts; turn = 20 sts

Row 5: (RS) Ch 1, sc in first st, sc in next 3 sts, [2 sc in next st, sc in next 3 sts] 3 times, sc in next 4 sts = 23 sts

Fasten off, leaving a long tail for sewing.

ADULTS – S, M, L

To beg: Ch 8

Row 1: (WS) Sc in second ch from hook (the skipped ch does not count as a st), sc in next 5 chs, 3 sc in last ch; working across the opposite side of the foundation ch, sc in next 6 chs; turn = 15 sts

Row 2: (RS) Ch 1 (does not count as a st now and throughout), sc in first st, sc in next 5 sts, 2 sc in each of next 3 sts, sc in next 6 sts; turn = 18 sts

Row 3: (WS) Ch 1, sc in first st, sc in next 5 sts, [2 sc in next st, sc in next st] 3 times, sc in next 6 sts; turn = 21 sts

Row 4: (RS) Ch 1, sc in first st, sc in next 5 sts, [2 sc in next st, sc in next 2 sts] 3 times, sc in next 6 sts; turn = 24 sts

Row 5: (WS) Ch 1, sc in first st, sc in next 5 sts, [2 sc in next st, sc in next 3 sts] 3 times, sc in next 6 sts; turn = 27 sts

Row 6: (RS) Ch 1, sc in first st, sc in next 5 sts, [2 sc in next st, sc in next 4 sts] 3 times, sc in next 6 sts = 30 sts

Fasten off, leaving a long tail for sewing.

Ears

Make 2 for each slipper.
Work in rows with **CC1** and a
4.25mm (G) hook.

KIDS – S, M, L

To beg: Ch 5

Row 1: (WS) Hdc in second ch from hook (the skipped ch does not count as a st), hdc in next 2 chs, 4 hdc in last ch; working across the opposite side of the foundation ch, hdc in next 3 chs; turn = 10 sts

Row 2: (RS) Ch 1 (does not count as a st), sc in first st, sc in next 2 sts, 2 sc in each of next 4 sts, sc in next 3 sts = 14 sts

Fasten off, leaving a long tail for sewing.

ADULTS – S, M, L

To beg: Ch 7

Row 1: (WS) Dc in fourth ch from hook (3 skipped chs count as dc), dc in next 2 chs, 6 dc in last ch; working across the opposite side of the foundation ch, dc in next 4 chs; turn = 14 sts

Row 2: (RS) Ch 1 (does not count as a st), sc in first st, sc in next 3 sts, 2 sc in each of next 6 sts, sc in next 4 sts = 20 sts

Fasten off, leaving a long tail for sewing.

FACE
Kids – S, M, L

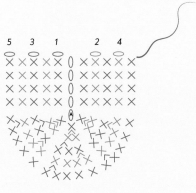

FACE
Adults – S, M, L

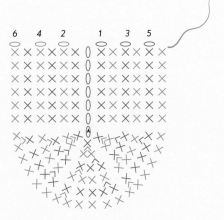

EAR
Kids – S, M, L

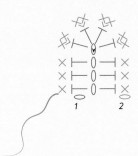

EAR
Adults – S, M, L

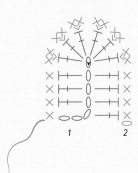

Hair

Make 1 for each slipper.
Work in rows with **MC** and a
4.25mm (G) hook.

KIDS – S, M, L

To beg: Ch 13

Row 1: (RS) Sc in second ch from
hook (the skipped ch does not
count as a st), sc in each ch across;
turn = 12 sts

Row 2: (WS) Ch 1 (does not count
as a st now and throughout), lp in
first st, lp in each st across; turn =
12 sts

Row 3: (RS) Ch 1, sc in first st, sc in
each st across; turn = 12 sts

Row 4: Same as Row 2

Fasten off, leaving a long tail
for sewing.

ADULTS – S, M, L

To beg: Ch 15

Row 1: (RS) Sc in second ch from
hook (the skipped ch does not
count as a st), sc in each ch across;
turn = 14 sts

Row 2: (WS) Ch 1 (does not count
as a st now and throughout), lp in
first st, lp in each st across; turn =
14 sts

Row 3: (RS) Ch 1, sc in first st, sc in
each st across; turn = 14 sts

Rows 4 – 5: Repeat Rows 2–3

Row 6: Same as Row 2

Fasten off, leaving a long tail
for sewing.

HAIR
Kids – S, M, L

HAIR
Adults – S, M, L

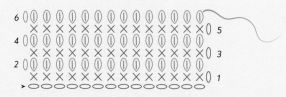

Finishing Slippers

To finish the eyes, use 10mm buttons for Kids' sizes or 15mm buttons for Adults' sizes. Place the buttons 3 sts below the top edge of the face **(fig 1)** and sew them on (*see Useful Information: Sewing Buttons*).

Thread the tapestry needle with **CC2** and stitch a Y-shaped nose onto face (*see Useful Information: Sewing Techniques*). Fasten off and weave in the end.

Position the face on the front of the slipper. Using the long **CC1** tail from the face, whipstitch across the top straight edge and backstitch around the curved edge onto the slipper **(fig 2)**. Fasten off and weave in the end.

Fold the ears in half and whipstitch across the raw edges using the long **CC1** tail from each ear **(fig 3)**. Position the ears on each side of the face and whipstitch around the edge onto the slipper using the long **CC1** tail from each ear **(figs 4 and 5)**. Fasten off and weave in the ends.

Position the hair along the top edge of the face and whipstitch around onto the slipper using the long **MC** tail **(fig 6)**. Fasten off and weave in the end.

3 sts below

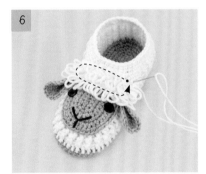

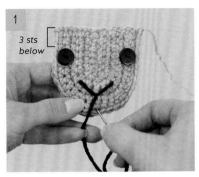

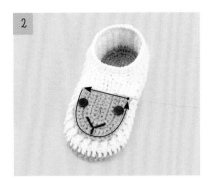

the Sandy Turtle

Like hard shells protect turtles as a shield, these comfy slippers will protect your toes from getting chilly. Sandy turtles are fun and colorful, so you can easily improvise by using your own favorite colors to make them.

Materials

YARN - WEIGHT 4
A small amount of **CC1** (Yellow), **CC2** (Dark Green), **CC3** (Brown), **CC4** (Clover Green) for turtle, or use your own colors.

Use **MC** (Warm Brown) for the upper of your slippers and outsoles, and use **CC4** (Clover Green) for insoles, or use your own colors.

HOOK
4.25mm (G)

ADDITIONAL MATERIALS
- Pins
- Tapestry needle and scissors

STITCH SUMMARY
Ch, sl st, sc, dc, tr, beg PC, PC, join

SKILLS
Working in the round, increasing, sewing

Skill Level
●●●○

Turtle

Make 1 for each slipper. Work in the round with a 4.25mm (G) hook, changing colors in every round as indicated.

KIDS – S, M, L

To beg: With **CC1**, ch 3, sl st in third ch from hook to form a ring (or start with a magic ring)

Rnd 1: Ch 1 (does not count as a st now and throughout), 6 sc in ring; break off **CC1** and join, changing to **CC2** = 6 sts

Rnd 2: With **CC2**, beg PC in same st as join, ch 2, [PC in next st, ch 2] 5 times; break off **CC2** and join, changing to **CC3** = 6 PC and 6 ch-2 sps

Rnd 3: With **CC3**, ch 2 (does not count as a st), skip st with join, 4 dc in next ch-2 sp, [skip PC, 4 dc in next ch-2 sp] 5 times; break off **CC3** and join, changing to **CC4** = 24 sts

Rnd 4: With **CC4**, ch 1, sc in same st as join; ch 5, dc in fourth ch from hook, dc in next ch (leg is made); *skip st of working rnd, sc in next 5 sts; ch 5, dc in fourth ch from hook, dc in next ch (leg is made)**; skip st, sc in next st, skip st, 6 dc in next st, skip st, sc in next st (head is made); ch 5, dc in fourth ch from hook, dc in next ch (leg is made); repeat from * to **; skip st of working rnd, sc in next 2 sts, sc in next st, ch 3, sl st in third ch from hook, sc in same st of working rnd (tail is made); sc in last st; join = 4 legs, 1 head and 1 tail

Fasten off, leaving a long **CC4** tail for sewing. Weave in all the other ends.

ADULTS – S, M, L

To beg: With **CC1**, ch 3, sl st in third ch from hook to form a ring (or start with a magic ring)

Rnd 1: Ch 2 (does not count as a st now and throughout), 12 dc in ring; break off **CC1** and join, changing to **CC2** = 12 sts

Rnd 2: With **CC2**, beg PC in same st as join, ch 2, dc in next st, ch 2, [PC in next st, ch 2, dc in next st, ch 2] 5 times; break off **CC2** and join, changing to **CC3** = 6 PC, 6 dc and 12 ch-2 sps

Rnd 3: With **CC3**, ch 2, skip st with join, 3 dc in next ch-2 sp, [skip st, 3 dc in next ch-2 sp] 11 times; break off **CC3** and join, changing to **CC4** = 36 sts

Rnd 4: With **CC4**, ch 1 (does not count as a st), sc in same st as join; ch 6, dc in fourth ch from hook, dc in next 2 chs (leg is made); *skip st of working rnd, sc in next 9 sts; ch 6, dc in fourth ch from hook, dc in next 2 chs (leg is made)**; skip st, sc in next st, skip 2 sts, 7 tr in next st, skip 2 sts, sc in next st (head is made); ch 6, dc in fourth ch from hook, dc in next 2 chs (leg is made); repeat from * to **; skip st of working rnd, sc in next 3 sts, sc in next st, ch 4, sl st in fourth ch from hook, sc in same st of working rnd (tail is made); sc in next 2 sts; join = 4 legs, 1 head and 1 tail

Fasten off, leaving a long **CC4** tail for sewing. Weave in all the other ends.

Finishing Slippers

Position the turtle on the front of the slipper and pin it around. Pins will help you to prevent shifting while sewing. Remove them as you sew. Using the long **CC4** tail from the turtle, backstitch onto the slipper around the body and head, leaving the legs and tail unstitched (**fig 1**). If needed, you can make a few whipstitches between the legs and the body to conceal the skipped st spaces. Fasten off and weave in the end.

1

TURTLE
Kids – S, M, L

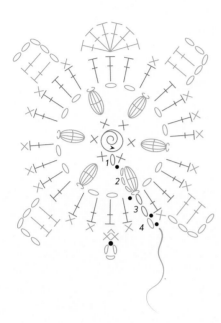

TURTLE
Adults – S, M, L

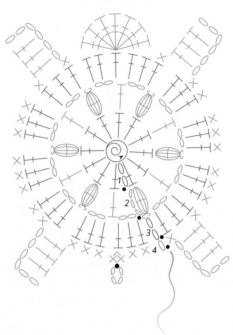

Tip

Use any desired colors to achieve a different appearance for your very own Sandy Turtles.

the Sassy Cat

★ ★ ★ ★ ★ ★ ★ ★ ★ ★ ★ ★ ★ ★ ★ ★ ★

When you feel like a cat and look like a cat, you will enjoy playing with yarn even more. With sassy cats on your feet, it's easy to take a nap and dream about yarn for a bit.

Materials

YARN - WEIGHT 4

A small amount of **MC** (Honey) for outer ears and hair, **CC1** (Light Pink) for inner ears and nose, **CC2** (Natural White) for muzzle, **CC3** (Black) for eyes.

Use **MC** (Honey) for the upper of your slippers and outsoles, and use **CC3** (Black) for insoles.

HOOK

4.25mm (G)

ADDITIONAL MATERIALS

- Stitch marker
- Tapestry needle and scissors

STITCH SUMMARY

Ch, sl st, sc, magic ring (optional)

SKILLS

Working in rows and in the round, increasing, sewing

Skill Level

● ○ ○ ○

Muzzle

Make 1 for each slipper. Work in spiral rounds with **CC2** and a 4.25mm (G) hook. Use a stitch marker to mark the start of each round as you go.

KIDS – S, M, L

To beg: Ch 3, sl st in third ch from hook to form a ring (or start with a magic ring)

Rnd 1: Ch 1 (does not count as a st), 6 sc in ring; do not join now and throughout = 6 sts

Rnd 2: 2 sc in first st of previous rnd, 2 sc in each of next 5 sts = 12 sts

Rnd 3: [Sc in next st, 2 sc in next st] 6 times = 18 sts

Sl st in next st and fasten off, leaving a long tail for sewing.

ADULTS – S, M, L

To beg: Ch 3, sl st in third ch from hook to form a ring (or start with a magic ring)

Rnds 1 – 2: Same as for Kids

Rnd 3: 2 sc in each st around = 24 sts

Rnd 4: Sc in each st around = 24 sts

Sl st in next st and fasten off, leaving a long tail for sewing.

Ears

Make 2 for each slipper. Work in rows with a 4.25mm (G) hook.

KIDS – S, M, L

INNER EAR:
For each ear, make 1 inner ear using **CC1**.

To beg: Ch 2

Row 1: 3 sc in second ch from hook (the skipped ch does not count as a st); turn = 3 sts

Row 2: Ch 1 (does not count as a st now and throughout), 2 sc in first st, 3 sc in next st, 2 sc in last st = 7 sts

Fasten off and weave in the ends.

OUTER EAR:
For each ear, make 1 outer ear using **MC**. Work same as inner ear but do not fasten off. Turn and proceed to joining row.

JOINING ROW:
Place the inner ear on top of the outer ear with WS facing each other and work the next row through both pieces at the same time, using the working yarn from the outer ear.

Row 3: (RS) Ch 1, 2 sc in first st, sc in next 2 sts, 3 sc in next st, sc in next 2 sts, 2 sc in last st = 11 sts

Fasten off, leaving a long tail for sewing.

MUZZLE
Kids – S, M, L

MUZZLE
Adults – S, M, L

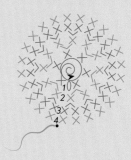

EAR
Kids – S, M, L

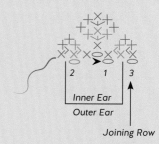

EAR
Adults – S, M, L

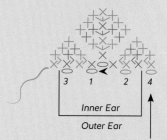

ADULTS – S, M, L

INNER EAR:

For each ear, make 1 inner ear using **CC1**.

To beg: Ch 2

Rows 1 – 2: Same as for Kids, turn

Row 3: Ch 1, 2 sc in first st, sc in next 2 sts, 3 sc in next st, sc in next 2 sts, 2 sc in last st = 11 sts

Fasten off and weave in the ends.

OUTER EAR:

For each ear, make 1 outer ear using **MC**. Work same as inner ear but do not fasten off. Turn and proceed to joining row.

JOINING ROW:

Place the inner ear on top of the outer ear with WS facing each other and work the next row through both pieces at the same time, using the working yarn from the outer ear.

Row 4: (RS) Ch 1, 2 sc in first st, sc in next 4 sts, 3 sc in next st, sc in next 4 sts, 2 sc in last st = 15 sts

Fasten off, leaving a long tail for sewing.

Finishing Slippers

Position the muzzle on the front of the slipper and backstitch around onto the slipper using the long **CC2** tail **(fig 1)**. Fasten off and weave in the end.

Thread the tapestry needle with **CC1** and stitch a T-shaped nose on the muzzle (*see Useful Information: Sewing Techniques*). Fasten off and weave in the end.

Thread the tapestry needle with **CC3** and stitch smiley eyes on each side of the muzzle (*see Useful Information: Sewing Techniques*), placing the inner edge of each eye by the gusset seam **(fig 1)**. Fasten off and weave in the ends.

Using the gusset seams as guides, position the ears 1 row into the gusset seams **(fig 2)**.

Whipstitch the ears around the bottom edge, using the long **MC** tail from each ear **(fig 3)**. Fasten off and weave in the ends.

To finish hair, wrap **MC** yarn 5 times around 4 fingers and cut the wraps on 1 side. Insert the hook through the stitches of the gusset between the ears, fold the yarn bundle in half and pull it through, creating a loop **(fig 4)**. Pull the yarn ends through the loop and tighten them. Trim off the ends to desired length.

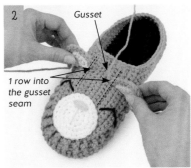

Gusset

Gusset

1 row into the gusset seam

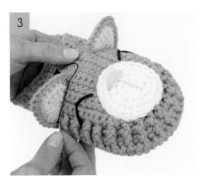

the Hippie Llama

- - - - - - - -

Llamas are the hippies of the animal kingdom. There is no time for drama when you can lay back and chill out with these comfortable llama slippers on your feet.

Materials

YARN - WEIGHT 4

A small amount of **MC** (Oatmeal) for ears and hair, **CC1** (Taupe) for nose, colorful yarn scraps for tassels (optional).

Use **MC** (Oatmeal) for the upper of your slippers, **CC1** (Taupe) for outsoles, and **CC2** (Light Pink) for insoles.

HOOK

4.25mm (G)

ADDITIONAL MATERIALS

- Buttons for eyes: 4 x 15mm for Kids S (M, L) or 4 x 20mm for Adults S (M, L)
- Sewing needle and thread
- Tapestry needle and scissors

STITCH SUMMARY

Ch, sc

SKILLS

Working in rows, working across the opposite side of the foundation chain, increasing, sewing

Skill Level

●○○○

Ears

Make 2 for each slipper. Work in rows with **MC** and a 4.25mm (G) hook.

KIDS – S, M, L

To beg: Ch 4

Row 1: (RS) Sc in second ch from hook (the skipped ch does not count as a st), sc in next ch, 3 sc in last ch; working across the opposite side of the foundation ch, sc in next 2 chs; turn = 7 sts

Row 2: (WS) Ch 1 (does not count as a st now and throughout), sc in first st, sc in next st, 2 sc in next st, 3 sc in next st, 2 sc in next st, sc in next 2 sts; turn = 11 sts

Row 3: (RS) Ch 1, sc in first st, sc in next 3 sts, 2 sc in next st, 3 sc in next st, 2 sc in next st, sc in next 4 sts = 15 sts

Fasten off, leaving a long tail for sewing.

ADULTS – S, M, L

To beg: Ch 5

Row 1: (WS) Sc in second ch from hook (the skipped ch does not count as a st), sc in next 2 chs, 3 sc in last ch; working across the opposite side of the foundation ch, sc in next 3 chs; turn = 9 sts

Row 2: (RS) Ch 1 (does not count as a st now and throughout), sc in first st, sc in next 2 sts, 2 sc in next st, 3 sc in next st, 2 sc in next st, sc in next 3 sts; turn = 13 sts

Row 3: (WS) Ch 1, sc in first st, sc in next 4 sts, 2 sc in next st, 3 sc in next st, 2 sc in next st, sc in next 5 sts = 17 sts

Row 4: (RS) Ch 1, sc in first st, sc in next 6 sts, 2 sc in next st, 3 sc in next st, 2 sc in next st, sc in next 7 sts = 21 sts

Fasten off, leaving a long tail for sewing.

Finishing Slippers

Thread the tapestry needle with **CC1** and stitch a Y-shaped nose (*see Useful Information: Sewing Techniques*), using the gusset curve as a guide **(fig 1)**.

To finish the eyes, use 15mm buttons for Kids' sizes or 20mm buttons for Adults' sizes. Sew the buttons on each side of the gusset seams (*see Useful Information: Sewing Buttons*), placing them just above the nose **(fig 1)**. Fasten off and weave in the ends.

Fold the ears in half and whipstitch across the raw edges using the long **MC** tail from each ear **(fig 2)**. Do not fasten off yet. Position the ears on each side of the gusset seams above the eyes **(fig 3)** and whipstitch onto slipper around the bottom edge, using the long **MC** tail from each ear **(fig 4)**. Fasten off and weave in the ends.

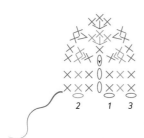

EAR
Kids – S, M, L

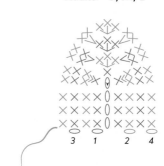

EAR
Adults – S, M, L

To finish hair, prepare 3 bundles of **MC** yarn with 5 strands in each bundle: Wrap yarn 5 times around 4 fingers and cut the wraps on 1 side (1 bundle made).

Insert the hook through the stitches of the center row of the gusset, fold the yarn bundle in half and pull it through, creating a loop **(fig 5)**. Pull the yarn ends through the loop and tighten them (first tassel made). Attach the second and third tassels in the same manner, placing them on each side of the first tassel. Trim the ends to desired length **(fig 6)**.

You can also add multicolored tassels around the ankles of your shoes and boots, but skip this step if you are making slides.

Cut the yarn bundles as needed by wrapping colorful yarn of your choice 3 times around 4 fingers and cutting the wraps on 1 side.

Finish the tassels in the same manner as hair, attaching them around the post of bpdc sts of the ankle side **(fig 7)**. Trim the tassels at the level of the sole **(fig 8)**.

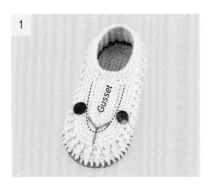

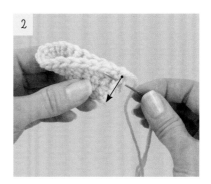

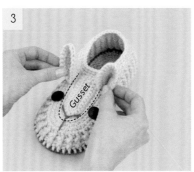

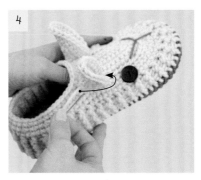

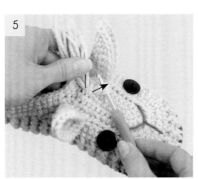

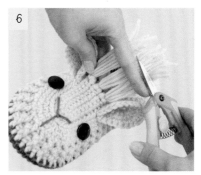

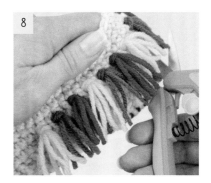

the Brave Moose

· · · · · · · · · · · · · · ·

Be brave, be strong and dream big with cozy moose slippers on your feet. If you're having a rough day, don't worry, nobody messes with a moose.

Materials

YARN - WEIGHT 4

A small amount of **MC** (Taupe) for ears, **CC1** (Beige) for muzzle, **CC2** (Chocolate) for antlers.

Use **MC** (Taupe) for the upper of your slippers and outsoles, and use **CC1** (Beige) for insoles.

HOOK

4.25mm (G)

ADDITIONAL MATERIALS

· Stitch marker
· Buttons for eyes: 4 x 10mm for Kids S (M, L) or 4 x 15mm for Adults S (M, L)
· Polyester stuffing
· Sewing needle and thread
· Tapestry needle and scissors

STITCH SUMMARY

Ch, sl st, sc, hdc, dc, magic ring (optional), join

SKILLS

Working in rows and in the round, working across the opposite side of the foundation chain, increasing, sewing

Skill Level

Muzzle

Make 1 for each slipper. Work in the round with **CC1** and a 4.25mm (G) hook.

KIDS – S, M, L

To beg: Ch 7

Rnd 1: Sc in second ch from hook (the skipped ch does not count as a st), sc in next 4 chs, 3 sc in last ch; working across the opposite side of the foundation ch, sc in next 4 chs, 2 sc in last ch; join = 14 sts

Rnd 2: Ch1 (does not count as a st), 2 sc in same st as join, sc in next 4 sts, 2 sc in each of next 3 sts, sc in next 4 sts, 2 sc in each of next 2 sts; join = 20 sts

Fasten off, leaving a long tail for sewing.

ADULTS – S, M, L

To beg: Ch 8

Rnd 1: Sc in second ch from hook (the skipped ch does not count as a st), sc in next 5 chs, 3 sc in last ch; working across the opposite side of the foundation ch, sc in next 5 chs, 2 sc in last ch; join = 16 sts

Rnd 2: Ch 1 (does not count as a st now and throughout), 2 sc in same st as join, sc in next 5 sts, 2 sc in each of next 3 sts, sc in next 5 sts, 2 sc in each of next 2 sts; join = 22 sts

Rnd 3: Ch 1, sc in same st as join, 2 sc in next st, sc in next 5 sts, [sc in next st, 2 sc in next st] 3 times, sc in next 5 sts, [sc in next st, 2 sc in next st] 2 times; join = 28 sts

Fasten off, leaving a long tail for sewing.

Ears

Make 2 for each slipper. Work in rows with **MC** and a 4.25mm (G) hook.

KIDS – S, M, L

To beg: Ch 5

Row 1: (WS) Hdc in second ch from hook (the skipped ch does not count as a st), hdc in next 2 chs, 4 hdc in last ch; working across the opposite side of the foundation ch, hdc in next 3 chs; turn = 10 sts

Row 2: (RS) Ch 1 (does not count as a st), sc in first st, sc in next 3 sts, 2 sc in each of next 2 sts, sc in next 4 sts = 12 sts

Fasten off, leaving a long tail for sewing.

ADULTS – S, M, L

To beg: Ch 7

Row 1: (WS) Dc in fourth ch from hook (the skipped chs count as beg dc), dc in next 2 chs, 6 dc in last ch; working across the opposite side of the foundation ch, dc in next 4 chs; turn = 14 sts

Row 2: (RS) Ch 1 (does not count as a st), sc in first st, sc in next 5 sts, 2 sc in each of next 2 sts, sc in next 6 sts = 16 sts

Fasten off, leaving a long tail for sewing.

Antlers

Make 2 for each slipper. Work in spiral rounds with **CC2** and a 4.25mm (G) hook. Use a stitch marker to mark the start of each round as you go.

KIDS – S, M, L

SHORT PIECES: Make 2 for each antler.

To beg: Ch 3, sl st in third ch from hook to form a ring (or start with a magic ring)

Rnd 1: Ch 1 (does not count as a st), 6 sc in ring; do not join now and throughout = 6 sts

Rnd 2: Sc in first st of previous rnd, sc in next 5 sts = 6 sts

Rnd 3: Sc in each st around = 6 sts

Sl st in next st and fasten off. Weave in the end on the first piece, but leave a long tail for sewing on the second piece.

LONG PIECE: Make 1 for each antler.

To beg: Ch 3, sl st in third ch from hook to form a ring (or start with a magic ring)

Rnds 1 - 3: Same as for short pieces

Rnds 4 - 10: Sc in each st around = 6 sts

Sl st in next st and fasten off, leaving a long tail for sewing.

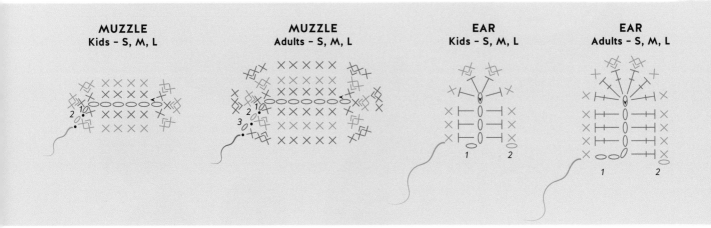

MUZZLE
Kids – S, M, L

MUZZLE
Adults – S, M, L

EAR
Kids – S, M, L

EAR
Adults – S, M, L

ADULTS – S, M, L

SHORT PIECES: Make 2 for each antler.

To beg: Ch 3, sl st in third ch from hook to form a ring (or start with a magic ring)

Rnd 1: Ch 1 (does not count as a st), 6 sc in ring; do not join now and throughout = 6 sts

Rnd 2: 2 sc in first st of previous rnd, sc next 2 sts, 2 sc in next st, sc in next 2 sts = 8 sts

Rnds 3 - 4: Sc in each st around = 8 sts

Sl st in next st and fasten off. Weave in the end on the first piece, but leave a long tail for sewing on the second piece.

LONG PIECE: Make 1 for each antler.

To beg: Ch 3, sl st in third ch from hook to form a ring (or start with a magic ring)

Rnds 1 - 4: Same as for short pieces

Rnds 5 - 12: Sc in each st around = 8 sts

Sl st in next st and fasten off, leaving a long tail for sewing.

Assembling Antlers

Whipstitch 2 short pieces across 2 stitches using the long **CC2** tail **(fig 1)**. Do not fasten off yet. Stuff all 3 pieces with polyester stuffing, then position the short pieces along the side of the long piece and whipstitch around using **CC2** tail **(fig 2)**. Fasten off and weave in the end.

Finishing Slippers

Backstitch a crooked smile on the muzzle using **CC2** and stitch the nostrils with **MC**. Fasten off and weave in the ends. Position the muzzle on the front of the slipper and backstitch around onto the slipper using the long **CC1** tail **(fig 3)**. Fasten off and weave in the end.

To finish the eyes, use 10mm buttons for Kids' sizes or 15mm buttons for Adults' sizes. Sew the buttons inside the gusset seams, placing them right up against the muzzle (*see Useful Information: Sewing Buttons*). Using **CC2**, backstitch a unibrow above the eyes **(fig 3)**. Fasten off and weave in the end.

Position the antlers on each side of the gusset seams **(fig 3)** and whipstitch around onto the slipper using the long **CC2** tail from each antler **(fig 4)**. Fasten off and weave in the ends.

Fold the ears in half and whipstitch across the raw edges using the long **MC** tail from each ear **(fig 5)**. Do not fasten off yet. Position the ears in front of the antlers, placing them 1 row away from the gusset seams **(fig 6)**. Whipstitch the ears around the bottom edge onto the slipper, using the long **MC** tail from each ear. Fasten off and weave in the ends.

Gusset

Gusset

1 row away from the gusset

the Artful Fox

Don't be shy to get a little crafty like a fox and make your very own artful fox slippers. It's a clever idea to make a few extra pairs as your whole family will enjoy them.

Materials

YARN - WEIGHT 4

A small amount of **MC** (Pumpkin) for outer ears, **CC1** (White) for face, **CC2** (Black) for inner ears, eyes and nose.

Use **MC** (Pumpkin) for the upper of your slippers, and use **CC2** (Black) for insoles and outsoles.

HOOK

4.25mm (G)

ADDITIONAL MATERIALS

• Tapestry needle and scissors

STITCH SUMMARY

Ch, sl st, sc, picot

SKILLS

Working in rows, raw edge finishing, increasing, sewing

Skill Level

Face

Make 1 left and 1 right piece for each slipper. Work in rows with **CC1** and a 4.25mm (G) hook.

NOTE:
For left-handed crochet, use the **LEFT PIECE** *instructions to make your right piece, and the* **RIGHT PIECE** *instructions to make your left piece.*

KIDS – S, M, L
LEFT PIECE

To beg: Ch 2

Row 1: (RS) 3 sc in second ch from hook (the skipped ch does not count as a st); turn = 3 sts

Row 2: (WS) Ch 1 (does not count as a st now and throughout), 2 sc in first st, 3 sc in next st, 2 sc in last st; turn = 7 sts

Row 3: (RS) Ch 1, 2 sc in first st, sc in next 2 sts, 3 sc in next st, picot, sc in next 2 sts, picot, 2 sc in last st, picot; do not turn = 11 sts and 3 picots

Edging: (RS) Rotate your work; ch 1, sc evenly across the bottom edge of the face, sl st in beg st of Row 3

Fasten off, leaving a long tail for sewing.

RIGHT PIECE

To beg: Ch 2

Rows 1 - 2: Same as for left piece

Row 3: (RS) Ch 1, sc in first st, picot, sc in same st, sc in next st, picot, sc in next st, (sc, picot, 2 sc) in next st, sc in next 2 sts, 2 sc in last st; do not turn = 11 sts and 3 picots

Edging: Same as for left piece

Fasten off, leaving a long tail for sewing.

ADULTS – S, M, L
LEFT PIECE

To beg: Ch 2

Row 1: (WS) 3 sc in second ch from hook; turn = 3 sts

Row 2: (RS) Ch 1 (does not count as a st now and throughout), 2 sc in first st, 3 sc in next st, 2 sc in last st; turn = 7 sts

Row 3: (WS) Ch 1, 2 sc in first st, sc in next 2 sts, 3 sc in next st, sc in next 2 sts, 2 sc in last st; turn = 11 sts

Row 4: (RS) Ch 1, 2 sc in first st, sc in next 4 sts, 3 sc in next st, picot, [sc in next 2 sts, picot] 2 times, 2 sc in last st, picot = 15 sts and 4 picots

Edging: (RS) Rotate your work; ch 1, sc evenly across the bottom edge of the face, sl st in beg st of Row 4

Fasten off, leaving a long tail for sewing.

RIGHT PIECE

To beg: Ch 2

Rows 1 - 3: Same as for left piece

Row 4: (RS) Ch 1, sc in first st, picot, sc in same st, sc in next st, picot, sc in next 2 sts, picot, sc in next st, (sc, picot, 2 sc) in next st, sc in next 4 sts, 2 sc in last st = 15 sts and 4 picots

Edging: Same as for left piece

Fasten off, leaving a long tail for sewing.

FACE
Kids - S, M, L

Left

Right

Sc across

Sc across

FACE
Adults - S, M, L

Left

Right

Sc across

Sc across

Ears

Make 2 for each slipper, using **CC2** for inner ears and **MC** for outer ears. Work in rows with a 4.25mm (G) hook, following the instructions from the cat slippers (*see The Sassy Cat: Ears*).

Finishing Slippers

Thread the tapestry needle with **CC2** and stitch a smiley eye on each piece of the face (*see Useful Information: Sewing Techniques*). Fasten off and weave in the end.

Position the left and right pieces of the face on the front of the slipper and backstitch around onto the slipper using the long **CC1** tail from each piece **(fig 1)**. Fasten off and weave in the ends.

Thread the tapestry needle with **CC2** and stitch a nose, inserting the needle several times through the inner corners of the face pieces **(fig 2)**. Fasten off and weave in the end.

Using the gusset seams as guides, position the ears 1 row into the gusset seams **(fig 3)**.

Whipstitch the ears around the bottom edge onto the slipper, using the long **MC** tail from each ear **(fig 4)**. Fasten off and weave in the ends.

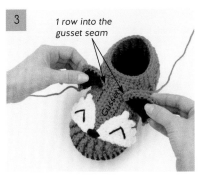

1 row into the gusset seam

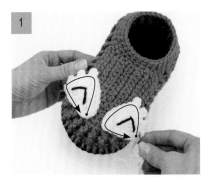

the Friendly Cow

- - - - - - - -

These friendly cows will keep your feet comfy when you enjoy a glass of milk before bed. They are also great in the morning when you need a little milk in your coffee.

Materials

YARN - WEIGHT 4

A small amount of **CC1** (Pretty Pink) for muzzle, **CC2** (Beige) for horns and nostrils, **CC3** (Black) for ears and spots, **CC4** (Terracotta) for hair.

Use **MC** (White) for the upper of your slippers, and use **CC2** (Beige) for insoles and outsoles.

HOOKS

4.25mm (G), 5.5mm (I)

ADDITIONAL MATERIALS

- Stitch marker
- Buttons for eyes: 4 x 15mm for Kids S (M, L) or 4 x 20mm for Adults S (M, L)
- Polyester stuffing
- Sewing needle and thread
- Tapestry needle and scissors

STITCH SUMMARY

Ch, sl st, sc, rsc, dc, tr, magic ring (optional), join

SKILLS

Working in rows and in the round, working across the opposite side of the foundation chain, increasing, sewing

Skill Level

●●○○

Muzzle

Make 1 for each slipper. Work in the round with **CC1** and a 4.25mm (G) hook.

KIDS – S, M, L

To beg: Ch 7

Rnd 1: Sc in second ch from hook (the skipped ch does not count as a st), sc in next 4 chs, 3 sc in last ch; working across the opposite side of the foundation ch, sc in next 4 chs, 2 sc in last ch; join = 14 sts

Rnd 2: Ch 1 (does not count as a st), 3 sc in same st as join, sc in next 4 sts, 3 sc in next st, sc in next st, 3 sc in next st, sc in next 4 sts, 3 sc in next st, sc in next st; join = 22 sts

Fasten off, leaving a long tail for sewing.

ADULTS – S, M, L

To beg: Ch 8

Rnd 1: Sc in second ch from hook (the skipped ch does not count as a st), sc in next 5 chs, 3 sc in last ch; working across the opposite side of the foundation ch, sc in next 5 chs, 2 sc in last ch; join = 16 sts

Rnd 2: Ch 1 (does not count as a st now and throughout), 3 sc in same st as join, sc in next 5 sts, 3 sc in next st, sc in next st, 3 sc in next st, sc in next 5 sts, 3 sc in next st, sc in next st; join = 24 sts

Rnd 3: Ch 1, sc in same st as join, 3 sc in next st, sc in next 7 sts, 3 sc in next st, sc in next 3 sts, 3 sc in next st, sc in next 7 sts, 3 sc in next st, sc in next 2 sts; join = 32 sts

Fasten off, leaving a long tail for sewing.

Ears

Make 2 for each slipper. Work in rows with **CC3** and a 4.25mm (G) hook.

KIDS – S, M, L

To beg: Ch 5

Row 1: (WS) Sc in second ch from hook (the skipped ch does not count as a st), sc in next 2 chs, 3 sc in last ch; working across the opposite side of the foundation ch, sc in next 3 chs; turn = 9 sts

Row 2: (RS) Ch 1 (does not count as a st now and throughout), sc in first st, sc in next 2 sts, 2 sc in each of next 3 sts, sc in next 3 sts; do not turn = 12 sts

Row 3: (RS) Ch 1, skip first st, rsc in next 10 sts, sl st in last st = 11 sts

Fasten off, leaving a long tail for sewing.

ADULTS – S, M, L

To beg: Ch 6

Row 1: (RS) Sc in second ch from hook (the skipped ch does not count as a st), sc in next 3 chs, 3 sc in last ch; working across the opposite side of the foundation ch, sc in next 4 chs; turn = 11 sts

Row 2: (WS) Ch 1 (does not count as a st now and throughout), sc in first st, sc in next 3 sts, 2 sc in each of next 3 sts, sc in next 4 sts; turn = 14 sts

Row 3: (RS) Ch 1, sc in first st, sc in next 3 sts, [sc in next st, 2 sc in next st] 3 times, sc in next 4 sts; do not turn = 17 sts

Row 4: (RS) Ch 1, skip first st, rsc in next 15 sts, sl st in last st = 16 sts

Fasten off, leaving a long tail for sewing.

Spots

Make 1 or 2 for each slipper. Work in the round with **CC3**, using a 4.25mm (G) hook for Kids' sizes or a 5.5mm (I) hook for Adults' sizes.

To beg: Ch 3, sl st in third ch from hook to form a ring (or start with a magic ring)

Rnd 1: Ch 3 (counts as first dc), (4 dc, 3 tr, 4 dc) in ring, ch 3, sl st in ring (counts as last dc) = 13 sts

Fasten off, leaving a long tail for sewing.

MUZZLE
Kids – S, M, L

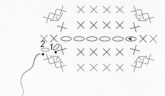

MUZZLE
Adults – S, M, L

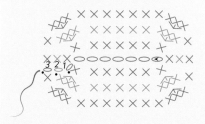

EAR
Kids – S, M, L

EAR
Adults – S, M, L

SPOT
All Sizes

Horns

Make 2 for each slipper. Work in spiral rounds with **CC2** and a 4.25mm (G) hook. Use a stitch marker to mark the start of each round as you go.

KIDS – S, M, L

To beg: Ch 3, sl st in third ch from hook to form a ring (or start with a magic ring)

Rnd 1: Ch 1 (does not count as a st), 6 sc in ring; do not join now and throughout = 6 sts

Rnd 2: Sc in first st of previous rnd, sc in next 5 sts = 6 sts

Rnds 3 - 4: Sc in each st around = 6 sts

Sl st in next st and fasten off, leaving a long tail for sewing. Stuff the horns.

ADULTS – S, M, L

To beg: Ch 3, sl st in third ch from hook to form a ring (or start with a magic ring)

Rnd 1: Ch 1 (does not count as a st), 6 sc in ring; do not join now and throughout = 6 sts

Rnd 2: 2 sc in first st of previous rnd, sc next 2 sts, 2 sc in next st, sc in next 2 sts = 8 sts

Rnds 3 - 6: Sc in each st around = 8 sts

Sl st in next st and fasten off, leaving a long tail for sewing. Stuff the horns.

Finishing Slippers

Thread the tapestry needle with **CC2** and stitch 2 nostrils on the muzzle, then position the muzzle on the front of the slipper and backstitch around onto the slipper using the long **CC1** tail **(fig 1)**. Fasten off and weave in the end.

To finish the eyes, use 15mm buttons for Kids' sizes or 20mm buttons for Adults' sizes. Sew the buttons on each side of the gusset seams (*see Useful Information: Sewing Buttons*), placing them right up against the muzzle **(fig 1)**.

Position the horns on each side of the gusset seams and whipstitch around onto the slipper using the long **CC2** tail from each horn **(fig 1)**. Fasten off and weave in the ends.

Fold the ears in half and whipstitch across the raw edges using the long **CC3** tail from each ear **(fig 2)**. Do not fasten off yet. Position the ears in front of the horns, placing them 1 row away from the gusset seams **(fig 3)**. Whipstitch the ears onto the slippers around the bottom edge, using the long **CC3** tail. Fasten off and weave in the ends.

Position the spot(s) as you like and backstitch onto the slippers around the edge using the long **CC3** tail **(fig 4)**. Fasten off and weave in the end.

Use **CC4** to finish the hair **(figs 5 and 6)**, following instructions from the llama slippers (see The Hippie Llama: Finishing Slippers).

the Roaring Lion

* * * * * * * * * * * * * * * * *

Do you enjoy roaring around the house and making fun things for your pride? These lion slippers will keep your royal cubs warm and able to pounce at a moment's notice, while still looking fierce.

Materials

YARN - WEIGHT 4

A small amount of **MC** (Gold) for ears, **CC1** (Beige) for muzzle, **CC2** (Taupe Heather) for mane, **CC3** (Chocolate) for nose.

Use **MC** (Gold) for the upper of your slippers and outsoles, and use **CC2** (Taupe Heather) for insoles.

HOOK

4.25mm (G)

ADDITIONAL MATERIALS

- Stitch marker
- Buttons for eyes: 4 x 15mm for Kids S (M, L) or 4 x 20mm for Adults S (M, L)
- Sewing needle and thread
- Tapestry needle and scissors

STITCH SUMMARY

Ch, sc, hdc, dc, lp

SKILLS

Working in rows and in the round, increasing, sewing

Skill Level

● ● ● ○

Muzzle

Make 1 for each slipper. To finish each muzzle, make 2 circles and sew them together. Work in spiral rounds with **CC1** and a 4.25mm (G) hook. Use a stitch marker to mark the start of each round as you go.

KIDS – S, M, L

To beg: Ch 3, sl st in third ch from hook to form a ring (or start with a magic ring)

Rnd 1: Ch 1 (does not count as a st), 6 sc in ring; do not join now and throughout = 6 sts

Rnd 2: 2 sc in first st of previous rnd, 2 sc in each of next 5 sts = 12 sts

Sl st in next st and fasten off, leaving a long tail for sewing when finishing the first circle and weave in the end of the second circle.

ADULTS – S, M, L

To beg: Ch 3, sl st in third ch from hook to form a ring (or start with a magic ring)

Rnds 1 - 2: Same as for Kids

Rnd 3: [Sc in next st, 2 sc in next st] 6 times = 18 sts

Sl st in next st and fasten off, leaving a long tail for sewing when finishing the first circle and weave in the end of the second circle.

FINISHING MUZZLE

Place 2 circles side by side and whipstitch across 3 sts using the long **CC1** tail from the first circle. Do not fasten off, but keep the long tail for future assembling.

Ears

Make 2 for each slipper. Work in rows with **MC** and a 4.25mm (G) hook.

KIDS - S, M, L

To beg: Ch 3, sl st in third ch from hook to form a ring (or start with a magic ring)

Row 1: (WS) Ch 1 (does not count as a st now and throughout), 4 hdc in ring; turn = 4 sts

Row 2: (RS) Ch 1, 2 sc in first st, 2 sc in each of next 3 sts = 8 sts

Fasten off, leaving a long tail for sewing.

ADULTS - S, M, L

To beg: Ch 3, sl st in third ch from hook to form a ring (or start with a magic ring)

Row 1: (WS) Ch 3 (counts as dc), 5 dc in ring; turn = 6 sts

Row 2: (RS) Ch 1 (does not count as a st), 2 sc in first st, sc in next st,

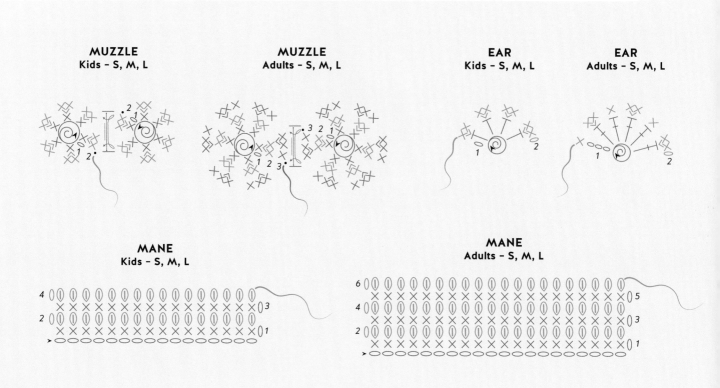

MUZZLE
Kids - S, M, L

MUZZLE
Adults - S, M, L

EAR
Kids - S, M, L

EAR
Adults - S, M, L

MANE
Kids - S, M, L

MANE
Adults - S, M, L

[2 sc in next st, sc in next st] 2 times = 9 sts

Fasten off, leaving a long tail for sewing.

Mane

Make 1 for each slipper.
Work in rows with **CC2** and a 4.25mm (G) hook.

KIDS – S, M, L

To beg: Ch 17

Row 1: (RS) Sc in second ch from hook (the skipped ch does not count as a st), sc in each ch across; turn = 16 sts

Row 2: (WS) Ch 1 (does not count as a st now and throughout), lp in first st, lp in each st across; turn = 16 sts

Row 3: (RS) Ch 1, sc in first st, sc in each st across; turn = 16 sts

Row 4: Same as Row 2

Fasten off, leaving a long tail for sewing.

ADULTS – S, M, L

To beg: Ch 21

Row 1: (RS) Sc in second ch from hook (the skipped ch does not count as a st), sc in each ch across; turn = 20 sts

Row 2: (WS) Ch 1 (does not count as a st now and throughout), lp in first st, lp in each st across; turn = 20 sts

Row 3: (RS) Ch 1, sc in first st, sc in each st across; turn = 20 sts

Rows 4 - 5: Repeat Rows 2–3

Row 6: Same as Row 2

Fasten off, leaving a long tail for sewing.

Finishing Slippers

Position the muzzle on the front of the slipper and backstitch around onto the slipper using the long **CC1** tail from the muzzle **(fig 1)**. Fasten off and weave in the end.

Thread the tapestry needle with **CC3** and stitch a T-shaped nose at the top edge between the circles of the muzzle (*see Useful Information: Sewing Techniques*). Fasten off and weave in the end.

To finish the eyes, use 15mm buttons for Kids' sizes or 20mm buttons for Adults' sizes. Sew the buttons on each side of the gusset seams (*see Useful Information: Sewing Buttons*), placing them right up against the muzzle **(fig 1)**.

Position the ears on each side of the loopy mane, approximately 1-2 st(s) away from the edges and between the first and second rows of loops. Using the long **MC** tail from each ear, whipstitch around the bottom edges onto the mane **(fig 2)**. Fasten off and weave in the ends.

Position your finished mane with its first row of loops above the eyes (front of the mane) and whipstitch around onto the slipper using the long **CC2** tail **(fig 3)**. Fasten off and weave in the end.

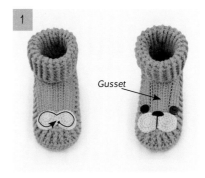

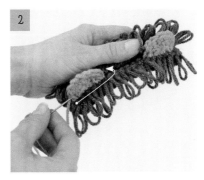

Gusset

Bonus Pattern

If you are just learning to crochet, try this beginner level pattern to make your first pair of slippers and then move up to the next level patterns. Use animal designs that are labeled for beginners to finish these basic slippers – Pug, Bear, Penguin, Koala, Sloth, Cat, Llama.

YARN: Medium weight (4)
HOOK: 5.5mm (I)
GAUGE: 14 sc x 16 rnds per 4 x 4in (10 x 10cm)
STITCH SUMMARY: Ch, sc, magic ring (optional)
SKILLS: Working in rows and in the round, raw edge finishing, increasing, sewing

1

WS

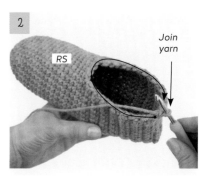

2

RS

Join yarn

3

Begin by working in spiral rounds with a 5.5mm (I) hook, using yarn colors recommended for the animal design you choose. Use a stitch marker to indicate the start of each round as you go.

Rnd/Row	KIDS			ADULTS		
	Small (S)	**Medium (M)**	**Large (L)**	**Small (S)**	**Medium (M)**	**Large (L)**
Beg	Ch 3, sl st in third ch from hook to form a ring (or start with a magic ring)					
1	Ch 1 (does not count as a st), 6 sc in ring; do not join now and throughout = 6 sts					
2	2 sc in first st of previous rnd, 2 sc in each of next 5 sts = 12 sts					
3	[Sc in next st, 2 sc in next st] 6 times = 18 sts					
4	Sc in each st around = 18 sts					
5	[Sc in next 2 sts, 2 sc in next st] 6 times = 24 sts					
6	Sc in each st around = 24 sts					
7	–			[Sc in next 3 sts, 2 sc in next st] 6 times = 30 sts		
8	–			Sc in each st around = 30 sts		
Next	Repeat Rnd 6 another 8 times	Repeat Rnd 6 another 9 times	Repeat Rnd 6 another 10 times	Repeat Rnd 8 another 10 times	Repeat Rnd 8 another 12 times	Repeat Rnd 8 another 14 times
	Continue to work the heel in rows					
1	(RS) Sc in each of next 22 sts; turn, leaving the remaining 2 sts unworked = 22 sts			(RS) Sc in each of next 28 sts; turn, leaving the remaining 2 sts unworked = 28 sts		
2	Ch 1 (does not count as a st), sc in first st, sc in next 21 sts; turn = 22 sts			Ch 1 (does not count as a st), sc in first st, sc in next 27 sts; turn = 28 sts		
Next	Repeat the previous row until the piece measures ½in (1.25cm) less than your foot length					

Fasten off, leaving a long tail for sewing. With WS facing you, fold the edge of the final row in half and whipstitch across **(fig 1)**. Fasten off and weave in the end, then turn your slipper right side out.

Edging: With RS facing, join yarn at the back seam and work sc evenly around the ankle edge; sl st in beg st to finish. Fasten off and weave in the ends **(fig 2)**.

Tip

When sewing on animal features, flatten out the front of the slipper to make it easier to position and sew the pieces **(fig 3)**. Sew through the top layer only, without catching the sole inside.

Additional Ideas

Mix 'n' Match Patterns

Let your creativity shine by mixing and matching patterns. Here are some starter ideas for ways to create new projects by combining separate features from different patterns. The possibilities are endless and I can't wait to see where your imagination takes you!

Uni-Cat

Uni-Cat is a mix of Unicorn and Cat. You can use the same concept to mix other animals with Unicorn. For example, try to make a Uni-Llama or Uni-Panda.

Make the muzzle and ears using the Sassy Cat pattern, then make the horn, stars and mane using the Starry Unicorn pattern. Finish the Cat's face with smiley eyes, and sew the horn in the center of the gusset above the face. Position and sew the ears in front of the horn, 1 row into the gusset seam **(fig 1)**. Finish hair the same as for the Sassy Cat. Use the 2 sets of mane spirals to create a tail for Uni-Cat **(fig 2)**. Position and sew on the stars as desired.

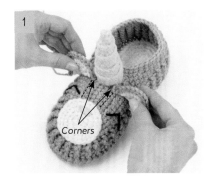

The Wise Owl

The Wise Owl is a combination of Penguin and Dinosaur.

Make the face using the Happy Penguin pattern but omit the buttoned eyes. Make 2 ears for each slipper from the Penguin's beak pattern, but using a 4.25mm (G) hook. And finally, make the beak using the horn pattern from the Zingy Dinosaur.

Sew the face onto the slipper in the same manner as for the Penguin. Position the beak in the center of the face, leveling up the top edge with the centers of the face circles. Using the long tail from the beak, whipstitch across the top edge and backstitch around the remaining edges **(fig 1)**. Using the same tail, stitch sleepy eyes across the center of each face circle (*see Useful Information: Sewing Techniques*). Fasten off and weave in the end.

Position the ears on each side above the face, slanting them to the sides. Using the long tail from the ears, whipstitch across the bottom edge, leaving the remaining edges unstitched. Make a few whipstitches 1 row below the top corner to secure the ears **(fig 2)**. Fasten off and weave in the ends.

Attach 2 tassels in the top corners of the ears and trim the ends short **(fig 3)**.

Useful Information

Terminology

The patterns featured in this book are written using abbreviations in American terms. Please use the comparison chart below to convert the patterns to British terminology if needed.

Abbreviation	Symbol	American (US) Term	British (UK) Term
Ch	○	Chain	Chain
Sl st	•	Slip stitch	Slip stitch
Sc	✕	Single crochet	Double crochet
Hdc	T	Half double crochet	Half treble crochet
Dc	✝	Double crochet	Treble crochet
Tr	✝	Treble crochet	Double treble crochet
		Skip	Miss
		Gauge	Tension

Abbreviations

This table explains all of the standard abbreviations and symbols used in this book.

Abbreviation	Symbol	Description in American (US) Terms
Arch	⌒5	Arch is a group of 3 or more chains as indicated in the pattern; when working in arch, insert the hook under the arch (and not into a specific chain), unless otherwise stated
Beg		Begin(ning)
Beg PC	⊕	**Beginning popcorn stitch** – Ch 3 (counts as dc), 4 dc in same st, remove the hook from the loop and insert hook from front to back through the top of beg ch-3, replace the loop onto the hook (from the last dc) and pull it through
Bpdc	Ŧ	**Back post double crochet** – Yo, insert the hook from back to front to back around the post of the stitch, yo and pull up a loop, [yo and pull yarn through 2 loops on the hook] 2 times
CC		Contrasting color (may be followed by a number if more than one is used in the pattern)
Ch(s)	⌀	**Chain(s)** – Yo and pull through the loop on the hook
Ch-		Indicates a number of chains or spaces previously made (example: ch-2 sp)
Cm		Centimeter(s)
Dc	T	**Double crochet** – Yo, insert the hook in stitch, yo and pull up a loop, [yo and pull through 2 loops on the hook] 2 times
Dc2tog	A	**Double crochet 2 together (decrease)** – [Yo, insert the hook in next stitch, yo and pull up a loop, yo and pull through 2 loops on the hook] 2 times, yo and pull through all loops on the hook
	V W	2 (3) dc in same stitch or space
	→ ➤	Direction indicators
Fasten off		Cut working yarn, draw the end through the loop on the hook and pull up tight
FLO		Front loop only – Work through front loop only when indicated
Fpdc	Ŧ	**Front post double crochet** – Yo, insert the hook from front to back to front around the post of the stitch, yo and pull up a loop, [yo and pull yarn through 2 loops on the hook] 2 times
Hdc	T	**Half double crochet** – Yo, insert the hook in stitch, yo and pull up a loop, yo and pull through all loops on the hook
In		Inch(es)
Join		Sl st in top of the first stitch, not a chain (*see Crochet Techniques*)
Lp(s)	◊	**Loop stitch(es)** – Holding yarn over your index finger, insert the hook in st and pass it over and behind the yarn to catch the far side of the working yarn, pull both strands through the stitch (3 loops on the hook); adjust the size of the loop to fit your finger circumference loosely, yo and pull through all 3 loops on the hook; release the loop off of your finger
M		Meter(s)
	◎	Magic ring or ch-3 circle
Marker	A	Stitch marker (indicated by a letter)
MC		Main color

Abbreviation	Symbol	Description in American (US) Terms
PC	(popcorn symbol)	**Popcorn stitch** – 5 dc in stitch indicated in the pattern, remove the hook from the loop and insert it from front to back through the top of the first dc, replace the loop onto the hook (from the last dc) and pull it through
Picot	(picot symbol)	**Picot** – Ch 3, insert the hook from right to left under the front loop and bottom vertical bar of previously made stitch (the base of the stitch), yo and pull through all loops on the hook
Rnd(s)		**Round(s)** – Work in a spiral or join the rounds, as indicated in the pattern
Row(s)		**Row(s)** – Turn after finishing each row, as indicated in the pattern
RS		Right side (front side of the item)
Rsc	(rsc symbol)	**Reverse single crochet (crab stitch)** – Insert the hook in stitch to the right from front to back, yo and pull it through, yo and pull through all loops on the hook (for left-handed crochet, insert the hook in stitch to the left instead of right)
Sc	×	**Single crochet** – Insert the hook in stitch, yo and pull up a loop, yo and pull through all loops on the hook
Sc2(3)tog	(decrease symbols)	**Single crochet 2 (3) together (standard decrease)** – [Insert the hook in next stitch, yo and pull up a loop] 2 (3) times, yo and pull through all loops on the hook. Or use invisible decrease (*see Crochet Techniques*)
	(increase symbols)	2 (3) sc in same stitch or space
	(seam symbol)	Seam
Shell	(shell symbol)	**Shell** is a group of stitches worked in same space – [2 dc, picot] 3 times, dc
Sl st	•	**Slip stitch** – Insert the hook in stitch, yo and pull through the stitch and loop on the hook
Sp		Space is a gap created by 1 or more chains; it might also be a space between 2 stitches or groups of stitches. Insert the hook into a chain space or in a space between stitches (not a specific chain or stitch)
St(s)		Stitch(es)
Tr	(treble symbol)	**Treble crochet** – Yo twice, insert the hook in stitch, yo and pull up a loop, [yo and pull through 2 loops on the hook] 3 times
WS		Wrong side (back side of the item)
Yd(s)		Yard(s)
Yo		Yarn over hook
	(wavy line symbol)	Yarn tail left for sewing
[ ]		Work the instructions written within brackets as many times as indicated after brackets
( )		Parentheses are used in explanations or to indicate a group of stitches and separate numbers for different sizes
* or **		Asterisks are used as reference marks
=		Equal sign indicates the total stitch count at the end of the row/rnd

Crochet Techniques

INVISIBLE DECREASE (SC2TOG)

Invisible decrease is a great shaping technique that allows you to avoid small gaps and bumps, generally created by the standard decrease method. It will help you to create a smooth and even texture while decreasing the gusset area of the slippers.

Invisible Sc2tog – [Insert the hook from front to back through the front loop of next st] 2 times **(fig 1)**, yo and pull through 2 front loops on the hook **(fig 2)**, yo and pull through the remaining 2 loops.

OPPOSITE SIDE OF FOUNDATION CHAIN

By working into both sides of the foundation chain, we create the beginning round (or row) of ovals, half ovals and other shapes.

Complete all of the required stitches, working in each chain across the foundation chain and place the increase stitches in the last chain **(fig 3)**. Rotate your work and crochet along the bottom loops of the foundation chain **(fig 4)**.

RAW EDGE FINISHING

To avoid gaps when working across the side stitches (raw edge), insert the hook through the stitches instead of working directly under the stitches **(fig 5)**.

JOINING ROUNDS

When you join rounds, insert the hook under the top loops of the first stitch, not a chain **(fig 6)**. Since the beginning chain does not count as a stitch, begin working each new round from the same stitch as join.

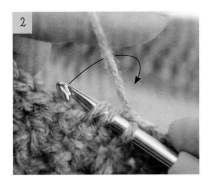

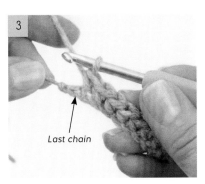

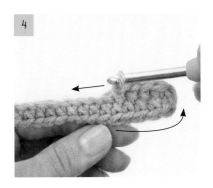

Last chain

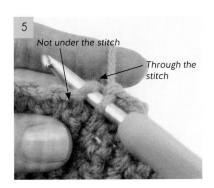

Not under the stitch

Through the stitch

SHORT ROWS

Using short rows is a very useful technique when it comes to creating 3-dimensional shapes without seams, such as Upper of Slides in this book. When working short rows, the pattern will direct you to work only a specific portion of the round, then turn and work back a specific number of stitches. Stitch markers will help you to track the beginning of short rows and you can remove them as you go.

WEAVING IN YARN ENDS

A neat finishing is the key to professional-looking work. To weave in the ends, thread the tapestry needle and run it through the stitches of the row on WS, approximately 1½in (3.8cm) away from the fastened stitch. Then turn and run the needle through the same stitches in the opposite direction, skipping the first stitch after turning. Turn and repeat weaving one more time for extra security if desired. Trim the remaining tail.

The patterns will specify whether you need to weave in the end when finishing or leave a long tail for sewing. However, always weave in the end from the beginning, unless otherwise indicated.

Care Instructions

Your slippers will last longer and will keep their shape if they are washed by hand. If you prefer using a washing machine, be sure to read the care instructions on the labels of all the materials used to select the correct temperature and cycle on your washing machine.

While some slippers are safe to wash on a low temperature gentle cycle, I highly encourage you **not to use** a washing machine for items that have dimensional add-ons, such as stuffed horns on the unicorn slippers or antlers on moose slippers. These items need to be washed by hand only.

How to hand wash:

- Fill a sink/basin with warm or cold water, depending on the temperature suggested on the materials label.
- Add delicate laundry detergent or dish soap.
- Submerge your slippers and soak them for 15-30 minutes.
- Gently squeeze your slippers without wringing to remove soapy water.
- Refill the sink/basin with fresh clean water and rinse your slippers gently. Repeat rinsing if needed.
- Squeeze water out and make a roll using a towel to absorb excess moisture.
- Lay your slippers flat on a clean dry towel and let them air-dry.

Do not tumble dry:

- If care label indicates that materials do not tolerate machine drying
- Slippers with non-slip soles made of shelf liner
- Slippers that were finished using fabric glue
- Slippers made of wool
- Slippers made of synthetic materials that may melt at high temperatures

Tip

You can use a drop of fabric glue on WS to conceal contrasting color ends and prevent them from showing on RS. Always test the glue before using.

Sewing Techniques

SEWING STITCHES

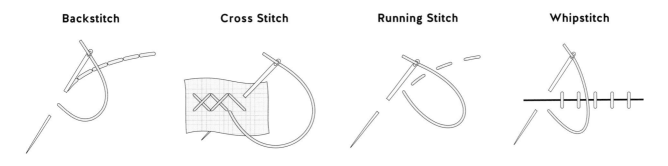

Backstitch **Cross Stitch** **Running Stitch** **Whipstitch**

STITCHING SHAPES

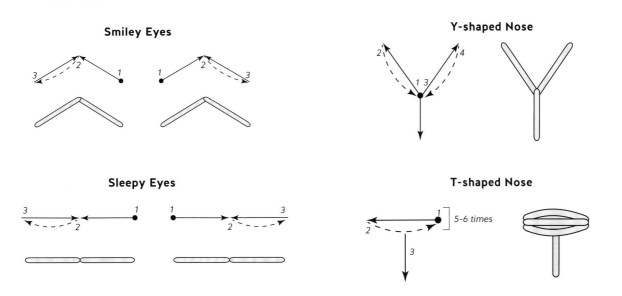

Smiley Eyes

Y-shaped Nose

Sleepy Eyes

T-shaped Nose

SEWING BUTTONS

To finish the animal eyes you will need:

- Flat buttons with 2 or 4 holes
- Strong all-purpose sewing thread
- Sharp sewing needle

Thread the needle, tie a knot at the end of the thread and you are ready to sew.

Some designs will specify to sew buttons onto an individually made piece that is not a part of a slipper yet (outer eyes, face, eye patches). In this case, position the button and hold it together with your crochet piece. Push the threaded needle up and down through the holes of the button and the fabric until it's securely attached **(fig 1)**.

If the eyes need to be sewn directly onto the slippers, it might seem difficult to pull the needle inside of the slippers, but don't worry, because it's not necessary. Here are a few helpful tips:

Position the eye as you like and secure your sewing thread in that spot of the slipper fabric. Pull the needle up through the first buttonhole, then push it down through the second buttonhole, catching the top layer of the slipper fabric under the button **(fig 2)**. Pull the thread all the way through and give it a tug. Now pull the needle up through the first buttonhole again **(fig 3)** and repeat the process until the button is securely attached.

There are also animals that use white craft felt for highlighting eyes (Pug, Panda, Raccoon, Monkey).

To prepare these eyes, sew the buttons onto a piece of felt with just a few stitches to keep them in place **(fig 4)**. Use sharp scissors to cut out a felt circle, by cutting around the button, slightly away from the edge **(fig 5)**.

Position and sew the eyes inserting the needle through the holes, felt and fabric **(figs 6 and 7)**, working in the same motion as described for sewing eyes without felt.

NOTE:
Buttons are not safe to use for small children. You can hand stitch the eyes using black yarn instead (see Sewing Techniques).

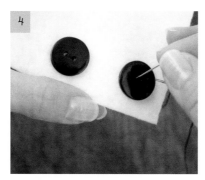

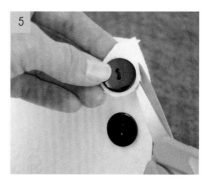

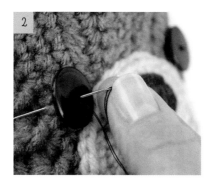

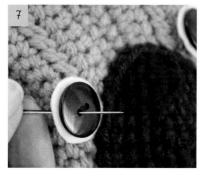

Tip

If your buttons have 4 holes, sew through 2 holes at a time, then repeat sewing through the remaining two holes.

USEFUL INFORMATION

Joining Gussets

Curves require very precise joining, which is essential to the final look of your slippers. Choose a joining method that suits your skill level and follow the steps carefully, without changing instructions, to prevent your slippers from shifting to the side.

WHIPSTITCH

Thread the tapestry needle using the long tail from the gusset. Sew 2 edges together, inserting the needle through front loops only (FLO) as follows:

SET-UP:

Pull the needle through the stitch with **Marker A** on the **slipper** and first stitch of the **gusset**, inserting it under FLO from **slipper** to **gusset**.

STEP 1:

Pull the needle through the next stitch of the **slipper** and **gusset**, inserting it under FLO from **slipper** to **gusset**.

Repeat Step 1, ending the last repeat in stitch with **Marker B** on the **slipper** and last stitch of the **gusset**.

Once finished, check to see whether your gusset is straight before weaving in the ends. If you missed a stitch by accident, it will cause slanting. Simply undo the seam and try again.

NOTE:
It's important to whipstitch through FLO as sewing through both loops might cause slanting.

FLO

Back loops

RIGHT-HANDED Whipstitch

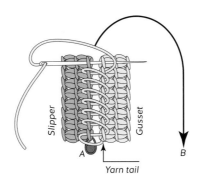

Slipper *Gusset*

A *B*

Yarn tail

LEFT-HANDED Whipstitch

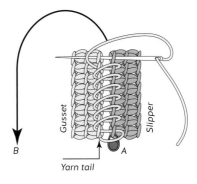

Gusset *Slipper*

B *A*

Yarn tail

SLIP STITCH

Using the long tail from the gusset and a 3.5mm (E) hook, crochet 2 edges together as follows:

SET-UP:

Sl st in stitch with **Marker A** on the **slipper**, inserting the hook under both loops from front to back.

Sl st in first stitch of the **gusset**, inserting the hook under both loops from front to back.

STEP 1:

Sl st in next stitch of the **slipper**, inserting the hook under both loops from front to back.

STEP 2:

Sl st in next stitch of the **gusset**, inserting the hook under both loops from front to back.

Repeat Steps 1 and 2, ending the last repeat in stitch with **Marker B** on the **slipper** and in last stitch of the **gusset**.

Once finished, check to see whether your gusset is straight before weaving in the ends. If you missed a stitch by accident, it will cause slanting. Simply undo the seam and try again.

diagrams on next page

RIGHT-HANDED Slip Stitch   ## LEFT-HANDED Slip Stitch

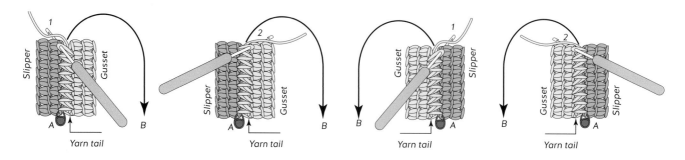

MATTRESS STITCH

Using the long tail from the gusset, thread the tapestry needle and sew 2 edges together as follows:

SET-UP:

Pull the needle through the stitch with **Marker A** on the **slipper**, inserting it under both loops from back to front.

Pull the needle through the first stitch of the **gusset**, inserting it under both loops from back to front.

STEP 1:

Pull the needle through the next stitch of the **slipper**, inserting it under both loops from back to front.

STEP 2:

Pull the needle through the next stitch of the **gusset**, inserting it under both loops from back to front.

Repeat Steps 1 and 2, ending the last repeat in stitch with **Marker B** on the **slipper** and in last stitch of the **gusset**.

Once finished, check to see whether your gusset is straight before weaving in the ends. If you missed a stitch by accident, it will cause slanting. Simply undo the seam and try again.

RIGHT-HANDED Mattress Stitch   ## LEFT-HANDED Mattress Stitch

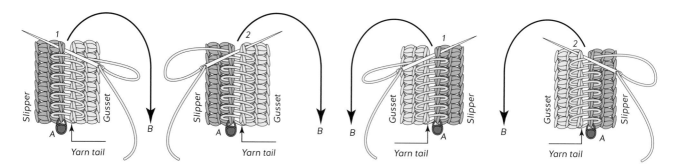

Left-Handed Crochet

If you are a left-handed crocheter, simply follow the exact same instructions, but working in the opposite direction. Work clockwise when you crochet in the round or from left to right when you crochet in rows. Left-handed crochet is a mirrored work of right-handed crochet. Here are a few mirrored images for making Shoes, Boots and Slides.

1. To work the joining round of your double-sole, join yarn in marker on the right instead of left **(fig 1)**.

2. With the outsole facing you, work the joining round and the upper of your slippers in a clockwise direction **(fig 2)**.

3. The long tail of the gusset will be on the opposite side compared to right-handed crochet; therefore, you will be sewing in the opposite direction **(figs 3 and 4)**.

4. Work the edging of Shoes, Boots and Slides as described but in the opposite direction **(figs 5 and 6)**.

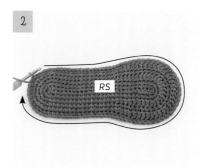

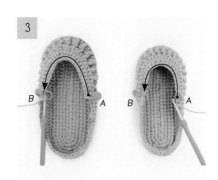

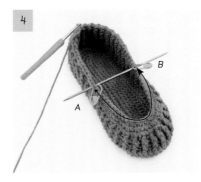

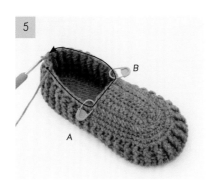

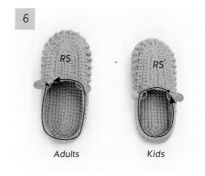

About the Author

Hi! I am a Canadian fiber artist, pattern designer and author. Coming from a family of textile engineers, I was surrounded by fabrics and yarn from the time I was born. Thus working with yarn has always felt natural to me.

I learned to knit and crochet at a very young age by watching my mom, grandma, and great-grandma. Over the years I learned new techniques and I developed some of my own.

My greatest passion is creating and writing fun patterns inspired by animals. I hope you will enjoy making animal slippers from this book and I would be thrilled if you check out my previous book *Crochet Animal Rugs*.

Thanks

A very special thank you goes to my testing team members for trying out, checking and proofreading all patterns from this book: Cheryl McNichols, Lenore Cartlidge, Ryan Nicole Hazeltine and Susan Baker. Also, thank you to my daughter Polina MacGarvey for editing the step-by-step photos.

Huge thanks to Yarnspirations for providing high quality yarn to everyone in my testing team and helping us to test all the animal slippers from this book. As always, it was a pleasure working with Bernat Super Value!

Suppliers

Bernat Super Value Yarn
www.yarnspirations.com
Red Heart Super Saver Yarn
www.yarnspirations.com
General Yarn
Canada: www.michaels.com
USA: www.joann.com
UK: www.hobbycraft.co.uk
Worldwide: www.lovecrafts.com
Stuffing, Buttons and Shelf Liner
Canada: www.walmart.ca
USA: www.walmart.com
Australia and New Zealand:
www.spotlightstores.com
Worldwide: www.amazon.com

Index

10 9 8 7 6 5 4 3

Publishing Director: Ame Verso
Managing Editor: Jessica Cropper
Project Editor: Rosee Woodland
Senior Designer: Sam Staddon
Photographer: Jason Jenkins
Pre-press Designer: Ali Stark
Art Direction: Prudence Rogers
Production Manager: Beverley Richardson

David and Charles publishes high-quality books on a wide range of subjects.
For more information visit www.davidandcharles.com.

Layout of the digital edition of this book may vary depending on reader hardware and display settings.